POWER
Prayers
for YOUR MARRIAGE

REBECCA CURRINGTON
VICKI J. KUYPER
PATRICIA MITCHELL

BARBOUR
PUBLISHING

Writing and compilation by Rebecca Currington, Vicki J. Kuyper, and Patricia Mitchell in association with Snapdragon Group℠.

ISBN: 978-1-60260-460-5

Published by Barbour Publishing, Inc., P.O. Box 719, Uhrichsville, Ohio 44683, www.barbourbooks.com

Our mission is to publish and distribute inspirational products offering exceptional value and biblical encouragement to the masses.

Member of the
Evangelical Christian
Publishers Association

Printed in the United States of America.

The Marriage Promise

Those who love me, I will deliver;
I will protect those who know my name.
When they call to me, I will answer them;
I will be with them in trouble,
I will rescue them and honor them.
With long life I will satisfy them,
and show them my salvation.

PSALM 91:14–16 NRSV

Contents

Introduction

$\mathcal{M}$arriage is a beautiful thing: the coming together of two souls, committed in love to each other. The wedding and the honeymoon are a wonderful time of celebration, and what lies ahead is a single path to be walked hand in hand. It is a cherished dream, something you both anticipated with great excitement as the day of your union approached. At last, you will each have a friend, a comrade, someone to whom you can give your love freely and trust completely.

Marriage is every bit of that and more on the earthly level, but it is also a spiritual bond of great importance to God. It is so important, in fact, that He uses the metaphor of marriage to describe His own relationship with those who accept His love and forgiveness. He calls Himself the bridegroom and the recipients of His grace and salvation His bride. What an amazing picture, and one He has laid out for us in the Bible.

In Ephesians 5:22–33, the Apostle Paul provides an overview of family leadership. "Wives, submit to your own husbands, as to the Lord. For the husband is head of the wife, as also Christ is head of the church; and He is the Savior of the body. Therefore, just as the church is subject to Christ, so let the wives be to their own husbands in everything" (NKJV).

This scripture has always been somewhat controversial. Some think it's calling for the suppression of women under the rule of their husbands. Others say the words are tainted and should be disregarded because of the male-dominant culture that influenced the writer. But in context, the passage tells us that Christ became the head of the church because of His willingness to sacrifice Himself completely for her. His regard for her—the church—leads Him to honor her as God's creation, offered to Him of her own free will and in response to His act of self-sacrifice. The Holy Spirit, through the pen

7

of the apostle Paul, asks wives to respect their husbands and honor them with the same earnest fidelity the Lord expects from His own bride.

Paul then addresses the presence of love in the marriage relationship and once again mirrors it after Christ's love for His church. "Husbands, love your wives, just as Christ also loved the church and gave Himself for her, that He might sanctify and cleanse her with the washing of water by the word, that He might present her to Himself a glorious church, not having spot or wrinkle or any such thing, but that she should be holy and without blemish. So husbands ought to love their own wives as their own bodies; he who loves his wife loves himself. For no one ever hated his own flesh, but nourishes and cherishes it, just as the Lord does the church. For we are members of His body, of His flesh and of His bones."

Paul explains that the marriage relationship has everything to do with love and nothing to do with power plays. Husbands are to love their wives more than they love their own bodies, willing to do whatever is necessary to protect, defend, and provide for them. Likewise, wives are to love their husbands and show their devotion by following their husbands' leadership.

Paul concludes by quoting from Genesis 2:24. He says: " 'For this reason a man shall leave his father and mother and be joined to his wife, and the two shall become one flesh.' This is a great mystery, but I speak concerning Christ and the church."

The beauty and magnitude of this passage should not be lost in a heated discussion of who should be doing what. Instead, it should be viewed through spiritual eyes. When Christ returns for His bride, the church, they will marry and stand from that day forward before God the Father as one. Earthly marriage mirrors this principle. Two people, bound by love, come together in a marriage ceremony, pledging their fidelity to one another before witnesses on earth and in heaven. The two become one flesh through their mutual partnership.

Marriage has gotten a bad rap in modern times. It is depicted more often as two opposing people than as the biblical ideal of two individuals coming together in a loving, respectful relationship. But the Bible's description is what God intended. His desire was for us to be reminded each and every day that His commitment to us is even stronger than the most durable earthly marriage, and that it is based on pure and holy love, a love that did not hesitate to make the ultimate sacrifice on our behalf. For you see, our earthly marriages are in fact designed to prepare us for our future role as the bride of Christ.

Are you wondering what this has to do with the power of prayer? The answer is, everything!

As husband and wife, you have entered into a union wholly sanctioned by God. He honors and exalts it. So greatly does He revere the bonds of matrimony that He urges husbands to live with their wives in understanding, honoring them, so that their prayers will not be hindered. (See 1 Peter 3:7.)

God wants to be a part of your relationship, and working together to create an intimate line of communication with Him can be a rewarding spiritual journey for you and your spouse. Imagine the spiritual power generated by two people praying together in such harmony and under the blessing and sanction of God. Their prayers would be multiplied exponentially. No matter what you are praying for: your country, your family, your health, your home, your church—even the affairs of God's kingdom—your prayers are potent and highly favored when you pray together as husband and wife. What an incredible privilege and responsibility!

The prayer models in this book are meant to guide and inspire you and your spouse as you discover the incredible length and breadth of all that God has to offer your marriage. They will help you create your own powerful prayers that seek, praise, and give thanks to the One who showers us with wisdom and unconditional love. As you read these scriptures and prayers, join hands and walk together before the throne of God—confident and filled with faith, knowing that you are heirs of His grace and peace.

Devote yourselves to prayer,
being watchful and thankful.

COLOSSIANS 4:2

Our Bible

The Power of Communication

A cord of three strands is not quickly broken.
ECCLESIASTES 4:12

*T*he Bible has been called many things: a historical document, a blueprint for morality, and the greatest book ever written. But on its most fundamental level, it is a love letter to each of us from our Creator and heavenly Father. Imagine Almighty God taking time to put down His thoughts and intentions for us to read. While it seems incredible, that's exactly what He did. Through the Holy Spirit, He divinely inspired individuals of His choosing to record His thoughts and intentions so that we would always know who He is and what His hopes and dreams are for us.

In a way, we are like adopted children receiving a letter from a birth parent. Though He created each of us, we didn't know Him personally right away. We first needed to understand all that had transpired between us, the nature of our alienation, and the terms of our redemption. We needed to know that He never turned from us; instead, we turned from Him. We also needed to understand how great and comprehensive His plan was to woo us back to Himself—not unlike the plan of a man to woo the woman he wishes to make his wife. All that and more is contained in His letter, the Bible.

As we read, we begin to see the truth about ourselves, about our world, and about our Father. The more we read, the more we are called to respond. Through prayer, we share our thoughts with Him and communicate freely and honestly. In this way, our relationship with God is rekindled.

Our relationship with God is a model for every aspect of marriage, and communication is no exception. Just as we must learn about God through the pages of the Bible, you and your spouse will need to open yourselves up to each other. You must each take time to share your brightest hopes and innermost fears, your dreams and disappointments, your worries and emotions. Once this happens, your lives can flow together in joyous union.

Make no mistake, the storms will come—and when they do, they can bring down the lines of communication between you and your spouse. No matter how much you love each other, there will always be days when you just can't seem to connect. God knows what that's like. He's been there. As you study the Bible together, you will learn how God got communication up and running again between Himself and us. His strategies for reconciliation—forgiveness, understanding, and healing—are all included in His letter so we can follow His example.

Is Bible study an integral part of your marriage relationship? If not, take time to find out what God has to say to you as a couple. Read a passage each day and then respond to His words by lifting your voices to Him in prayer.

A Worthy Example

Everything that was written in the past was written to teach us,
so that through endurance and the encouragement
of the Scriptures we might have hope.
ROMANS 15:4

*D*ear heavenly Father, thank You for loving us and going to such great measures to tell us so. Thank You for the scriptures that communicate all Your intentions for us, especially Your plan for our marriage. As we read Your words in the Bible and respond to You in prayer, we believe we will learn from Your example and find it easier to communicate with each other. We are grateful. Amen.

Better People

All Scripture is God-breathed and is useful for teaching, rebuking,
correcting and training in righteousness, so that the man of God
may be thoroughly equipped for every good work.
2 TIMOTHY 3:16–17

*D*ear Lord, we are so glad that the Bible shows us how to address those areas in our lives that we stubbornly refuse to change and teaches us how to submit ourselves to correction and become better people. This helps us not only in our relationship with You but also in our relationship with each other. Thanks for teaching us how to make our marriage better. Amen.

Holding Tight

*Keep your eyes open, hold tight to your convictions,
give it all you've got, be resolute.*

1 CORINTHIANS 16:13 MSG

*H*eavenly Father, life's challenges often lead us to a crossroads, and we sometimes have to choose between our desires and Your commandments. When we encounter these tough decisions, help us hold tightly to our faith, our convictions, and Your Word. Grant us the power to remain true to You and our marriage commitment in all things. Amen.

Sharing Your Word

*I make it my ambition to proclaim the good news, not where Christ has
already been named, so that I do not build on someone else's foundation.*

ROMANS 15:20 NRSV

*F*ather God, what an honor it is to carry the Good News of salvation to the world around us. Help us be sensitive to those around us who do not yet know what You have done for all of us. Then, Lord, give us opportunities to share our passion for Your Word as we proclaim the miracle of Your love and forgiveness. Amen.

The Light of Hope

*We have the word of the prophets made more certain,
and you will do well to pay attention to it,
as to a light shining in a dark place.*

2 PETER 1:19

*D*ear Father, it's easy for us to look around and see that marriage is a constant challenge. The failed marriage statistics are discouraging, and it's difficult sometimes to hope that we can beat the odds and keep our marriage strong. When we feel the darkness moving in, we will look to Your Word, the Bible, to help us keep the light of hope shining in our hearts. Amen.

Our Commitment

Do your best to present yourself to God as one approved, a workman who does not need to be ashamed and who correctly handles the word of truth.

2 TIMOTHY 2:15

*H*eavenly Father, Your words in the Bible encourage us to make our marriage more resilient—not just when our love is new and exciting but also as the years and realities of life begin to wear us down. We commit to worshipping You through prayer and Bible study so that one day we can look back and feel satisfied that we were good stewards of Your love. Amen.

Wisdom Is a Weapon

Whoever would love life and see good days must keep his tongue from evil and his lips from deceitful speech. He must turn from evil and do good; he must seek peace and pursue it.

1 PETER 3:10–11

*L*ord God, keep us strong in our words and actions. Give us hearts full of renewed strength so we may stand fast in our commitment to follow You. Do not let life's struggles turn us away from obedience, and show us how to use Your Word and Your wisdom as a weapon in our efforts to meet our challenges. Amen.

The Love Light Glowing

Jesus answered, "It is written: 'Man does not live on bread alone,
but on every word that comes from the mouth of God.'"

MATTHEW 4:4

*D*ear Lord, we used to think we could simply "live on our love," but like the bread that keeps our bodies going, the love that keeps our marriage going is simply not enough. We rely on You for true sustenance, Lord, and through Your Word, You have given us the stability and strength we need to keep the love light glowing. We thank You. Amen.

Going for the Glory

I consider that our present sufferings are not worth comparing
with the glory that will be revealed in us.

ROMANS 8:18

*H*eavenly Father, when we look at our challenges, we despair; but when we look to Your promises in the Bible, we rejoice. What great and wonderful things You have in store for us. Let each challenge that comes our way serve as a reminder for us to look to You and go for the glory! Amen.

Readiness in Ministry

In your hearts sanctify Christ as Lord. Always be ready to make your defense to anyone who demands from you an accounting for the hope that is in you.

1 PETER 3:15 NRSV

*H*eavenly Father, thank You for Your Word, our source of knowledge and spiritual wisdom. Motivate us to remain faithful students of scripture so we will be ready at all times to speak up for the gospel and answer those who question our trust in You. With Your Spirit at work in us, we minister in readiness and joy. Amen.

The Perfect Standard

The word of God is living and active. Sharper than any double-edged sword, it penetrates even to dividing soul and spirit, joints and marrow; it judges the thoughts and attitudes of the heart.

HEBREWS 4:12

*H*oly Father, You see our innermost thoughts and know all our secrets. As we study Your Word, help us come clean with You and with each other. We want to be holy and pure before You, both as individuals and as a couple. Thank You for giving us the Bible—the perfect standard for righteous living—and the grace to journey through it together. Amen.

Spiritual Weapons

Though we live in the world, we do not wage war as the world does.
The weapons we fight with are not the weapons of the world.
On the contrary, they have divine power to demolish strongholds.

2 CORINTHIANS 10:3–4

All-powerful God, You know the world is full of challenges to our faith, so You equip Your people with the spiritual weapons of Your Word, Your authority, and Your love. Prepare us for battle, dear God, and teach us to use our spiritual weapons to combat the challenges we face as believers and followers of Jesus Christ. Amen.

Common Understanding

*The unfolding of your words gives light;
it gives understanding to the simple.*

PSALM 119:130

*H*eavenly Father, we have come together as two people from different homes, different lifestyles, and different mind-sets. Though we love each other, we often find it difficult to establish a common understanding. We often confuse one another with our words and actions, but as we study Your Word together, we ask that You will enlighten our understanding of each other and of Your plan for our lives together. Amen.

The Laws of Peace

*Great peace have they who love your law,
and nothing can make them stumble.*

PSALM 119:165

*D*ear Father, the whole world is crying out for peace—peace between nations and even peace within homes. We long for peace as well, the kind of peace that comes from walking in step with each other and with You. Thank You for helping us learn the laws of peace and how to foster harmony in our marriage through Your Word. Amen.

Our Faith

The Power of Promise

[Abraham] did not waver through unbelief regarding the promise of God, but was strengthened in his faith and gave glory to God, being fully persuaded that God had power to do what he had promised.
ROMANS 4:20–21

*T*hink back to your wedding day. If you had a traditional ceremony, you stood before an altar, and as your friends and families looked on, you took each other's hands, looked deeply into each other's eyes, and promised to love, honor, and cherish one another until death. You sealed that promise with rings and a kiss.

On that special day, you probably never imagined how quickly, how often, or how thoroughly those promises would be tested. Marriage, it turns out, is *not* just one lovely romantic moment after another. The winds of life often disturb the waters of marital bliss, but through it all, God expects you to remain faithful. To do that, you must keep yourself focused not only on your promises to each other but also God's promises to you. Your faith in Him is truly the only way you can maintain your faith in each other.

The Bible defines faith in Hebrews 11:1 as "confidence that what we hope for will actually happen. It gives us assurance about things we cannot see" (NLT). When you give your heart and life to God and receive His salvation through His Son,

Jesus Christ, you promise to abandon your sin and live a life that is pleasing to Him. In exchange, He promises that He will no longer remember the past. He promises never to leave you. He promises to love you, listen to you, and do His best to make you happy always. And He promises that when you die, you will be with Him for all eternity. Faith is when you believe His promises, take them to heart, and live your life accordingly.

The same type of faith is needed in marriage. You and your spouse made promises to each other on your wedding day, and having faith provides that you will believe in those promises, take them to heart, and live your lives accordingly.

Wouldn't it be wonderful if your faith in God and your faith in each other never wavered? One day in heaven that will be the case, but while on earth, you will struggle at times to keep your faith intact. Ecclesiastes 4:9–12 says, "Two are better than one, because they have a good reward for their toil. For if they fall, one will lift up the other. . . . And though one might prevail against another, two will withstand one" (NRSV). Therefore, encourage each other in your faith. Pray together. And when you disappoint each other and God, follow His blueprint for restoration: humility, repentance, and forgiveness.

You can always call on God for help. He understands your challenges and your humanity and will never give up on you.

Pursuing Virtue

Pursue righteousness, godliness, faith,
love, endurance and gentleness.
1 TIMOTHY 6:11

*D*ear God, we know that a right relationship with You is imperative if we are to have a right relationship with each other. Help us avoid complacency and always pursue those virtues that are lovely and pleasing in Your eyes. Amen.

The Weapon of Humility

Do not think of yourself more highly than you ought,
but rather think of yourself with sober judgment,
in accordance with the measure of faith God has given you.
ROMANS 12:3

*H*eavenly Father, pride can extinguish our faith in You and in each other. When it rears its ugly head, quickly admonish us so that we may escape its danger. Keep us ever mindful that we have an enemy who wants to destroy our relationship with You and each other. Help us establish humility in our hearts and use its power to defend our faith and keep our marriage strong. Amen.

Prepared to Follow

*Said Jesus unto his disciples, If any man will come after me,
let him deny himself, and take up his cross, and follow me.
For whosoever will save his life shall lose it: and whosoever
will lose his life for my sake shall find it.*
MATTHEW 16:24–25 KJV

*D*ear Father, help us to be as strong and diligent as Your disciples, living our lives in harmony and for the purpose You created us. When we think we know better, gently nudge us and remind us that You know best. Amen.

God's Faithfulness

*Know therefore that the Lord your God is God, the faithful God
who maintains covenant loyalty with those who love him and
keep his commandments, to a thousand generations.*
DEUTERONOMY 7:9 NRSV

*A*wesome God, that's truly what You are. How is it that You care so much about us and want to be so involved in our relationship? We are humbled that You have diligently kept Your covenant with us. Our hearts are full of praise and thanksgiving to You for Your faithful, constant presence in our lives. Amen.

An Eager Ear

Faith comes from what is heard,
and what is heard comes through the word of Christ.
ROMANS 10:17 NRSV

*D*ear Lord, there are so many voices in the world, so many distractions, so many negative influences. Teach us how to distinguish Your voice above the fray. Then help us, Lord, to listen with great care to what You are saying to us. As we listen, we know our faith will grow. Amen.

A Receptive Heart

[Jesus answered them,]
"Whatever you ask for in prayer with faith,
you will receive."
MATTHEW 21:22 NRSV

*D*ear Father, thank You for Your great and mighty promises. There is nothing we could possibly want or need that You cannot provide for us. We are certain of that. Help us, though, to refrain from asking for what *we* want long enough to hear what *You* want for us. We don't always know what's best for us—but You do! Thank You for giving us the faith we need to believe that You hear and answer our prayers. Amen.

Moving a Mountain

[Jesus] replied. . . "I tell you the truth, if you have faith as small as a mustard seed, you can say to this mountain, 'Move from here to there' and it will move. Nothing will be impossible for you."
MATTHEW 17:20

*L*ord God, sometimes it seems like there's a mountain standing between us. Thank You for promising that we can come to You and gain the strength we need to move the mountain. No matter how high or how wide, You will always help us remove it so that we can maintain our love and commitment to each other. Amen.

True Victory

*Whatever is born of God conquers the world.
And this is the victory that conquers the world, our faith.*
1 JOHN 5:4 NRSV

*D*ear Father, just like most other couples, we have a strategy for succeeding in this world. Help us remember that no matter how well we do for ourselves, it's all for nothing if we lose our faith in You and in each other. That's where true victory lies. We pray for increased faith as we surrender our marriage to You each and every day. Amen.

Hearts that Seek God

*Without faith it is impossible to please God,
because anyone who comes to him must believe that he
exists and that he rewards those who earnestly seek him.*
HEBREWS 11:6

*D*ear Lord, we want more than anything to please You. Touch our hearts and lead us to Your wisdom, unveiling the next step of Your will for our lives. We offer our faith to You with grateful acknowledgment of Your power and influence in our lives. Thank You for Your promise to reward our faith with even more. Amen.

Sincere Hearts

*Let us draw near to God with a sincere
heart in full assurance of faith.*
HEBREWS 10:22

*H*eavenly Father, we know all too well the dangers of giving in to our own selfish thoughts and desires. When that happens, we become manipulative and insincere. Soon we find that we have drifted away from each other and away from Your loving presence. We ask that You would help us maintain sincere hearts that quickly respond to You. Amen.

Pure Garments

Those who are right with God will live by faith.
HABAKKUK 2:4 NCV

*H*oly Father, we ask that Your Holy Spirit would quickly admonish our hearts whenever we drift away from Your presence or fall into temptation and sin. It is our greatest desire to stand before You in pure garments of praise and thanksgiving. By faith we step forward, looking to You to help us keep ourselves clean and holy. Amen.

First Steps

*If people say they have faith, but do nothing,
their faith is worth nothing.*
JAMES 2:14 NCV

*D*ear Father, we understand that our faith must be used in order to serve a purpose. It must be strong enough for us to step out onto it, and we must be confident in its ability to uphold us. We know that our faith in You is never misplaced. Amen.

Steady, Faithful Hearts

*Those who are attentive to a matter will prosper,
and happy are those who trust in the LORD.*
PROVERBS 16:20 NRSV

*D*ear Lord, help us to quickly respond when You speak to our hearts—as quickly as Peter did when he left the boat to walk on water. We know that where faith is concerned, hesitation will rob us of the greatness You have planned for us. Give us steady, faithful hearts that are willing and ready to do Your bidding. Amen.

Gaining Confidence

*Faith is the confidence that what we hope for will actually happen;
it gives us assurance about things we cannot see.*
HEBREWS 11:1 NLT

*P*recious Father, thank You for the confidence we have each time we join hands and come together in Your presence. It is a comfort to know You hear us and that we are pleasing to You. We know You will answer our prayers, and we thank You for that blessed assurance. Amen.

Our Love

The Power of Sacrifice

Live a life of love, just as Christ loved us and gave himself
up for us as a fragrant offering and sacrifice to God.
EPHESIANS 5:2

According to the Beatles, all you need is love. A simple philosophy—but is it true? Is love really all husbands and wives need to sustain a fulfilling, long-term, God-honoring relationship? That depends a lot on how we define love.

In English translations of the New Testament, the word *love* is represented by four Greek words, each describing a different kind of love. *Phileo* is the endearing love shared by close friends. *Eros* relates to physical love. *Storge* describes familial love. *Agape* refers to the kind of love that is totally unconditional, the kind of love God lavishes on His children.

Marriage is the only relationship where all four of these words for love intersect—or at least where they should. While deep friendship, familial love, and physical affection are frequently shared between husbands and wives, agape love is often left on the sidelines. Yet agape is the kind of love human hearts long for most. That's because it's the kind of love that best reflects the heart of God.

Look at Jesus. Just before He was arrested, He told His disciples, "My command is this: Love [agape] each other as I have loved you. Greater love [agape] has no one than this, that he lay down his life for his friends" (John 15:12–13). Then

Jesus did just that—He gave up His life.

Sacrifice is at the core of agape love. But you don't have to die physically to love your spouse in a godly way. The time, possessions, comfort, or pride that you sacrifice can be given as agape gifts. In a marriage relationship, these gifts can be as small as washing your spouse's car or as large as forgiving a gut-wrenching offense.

Unconditional, self-sacrificing love is not a doormat kind of love. It knows how to give, but it also joyfully receives. It's motivated by compassion and care—not a sense of duty or the desire to "look" like a loving spouse. It can only take root through the power of God's Spirit.

By spending time with God in prayer and faithfully listening to His instruction, you'll discover all four types of love blooming more beautifully in your marriage. Love is more than a feeling. It is a conscious decision and an unexpected gift all at once. Ask God what gifts of love you can provide for each other today. Risk giving them freely, without obligation. As Ephesians 5:25–28 says in *The Message*, "Husbands, go all out in your love for your wives, exactly as Christ did for the church—a love marked by giving, not getting. . . . And that is how husbands ought to love their wives. They're really doing themselves a favor—since they're already 'one' in marriage." So, do each other a favor. Follow God's example by lavishly pouring out your love on one another.

The Grace to Forgive

He who covers over an offense promotes love.
PROVERBS 17:9

*D*ear Lord, no matter how hard we try, it seems like one of us is always saying or doing something that offends the other. Help us to think before we speak, remembering that our love is more important than our petty issues. And for those times when we do offend, give us the grace to forgive and cover each other with our love. Amen.

Loving Actions

Let all that you do be done in love.
1 CORINTHIANS 16:14 NRSV

*H*eavenly Father, sometimes we forget that actions speak louder than words. Point out to us when we are insensitive and hurtful to one another. Give us the grace to say we are sorry and the desire to amend our actions accordingly. Amen.

The Ways of Love

These three remain: faith, hope and love.
But the greatest of these is love. Follow the way of love.
1 CORINTHIANS 13:13; 14:1

*D*ear Father, we ask that You would teach us to follow the way of love when it comes to our relationship with You, with each other, and with all those You have placed in our lives. So often we say we love, but we follow paths that suggest otherwise. We want to speak love and show it as well. Amen.

A Prayer of Dedication

"Worship the Lord your God, and serve him only."
MATTHEW 4:10

*H*eavenly Father, we dedicate ourselves, our marriage, and our love for You and for each other to serving You with the blessings You have given us. We want to reach out to those who have not known the joys of Your love. Thank You for the privilege of working for You. Amen.

Bound Together

Bear with each other and forgive whatever grievances you may have against one another. Forgive as the Lord forgave you. And over all these virtues put on love, which binds them all together in perfect unity.
COLOSSIANS 3:13–14

Good Father, we once dreamed of married life, spending all our nights and days together. Now we know that living together and living in harmony are not always the same thing. Teach us the ways of unity—tolerance, forgiveness, and true selfless love. Amen.

Discovering Who We Are

It's in Christ that we find out who we are and what we are living for.
EPHESIANS 1:11 MSG

Creator God, You have graciously given us Your Word so we may come to know You as our Creator and Father. You have made us in Your image, and You have given us the blessing of love for each other. Now we pray that You would create in us hearts open to Your guidance and give us faith to follow You together as husband and wife. Amen.

Patient Restraint

Love takes no pleasure in evil but rejoices over the truth.
Love patiently accepts all things. It always trusts,
always hopes, and always endures. Love never ends.
1 CORINTHIANS 13:6–8 NCV

*H*eavenly Father, we want to love each other so deeply that we are never even tempted to hurt each other with our words or actions. We want always to be truthful and honest with each other. We ask for the patience to reach that place in our relationship. Thank You for planting a true and eternal love in our hearts for You and for each other. Amen.

Love One Another

*[Jesus said,] "A new command I give you: Love one another.
As I have loved you, so you must love one another. By this all
men will know that you are my disciples, if you love one another."*
JOHN 13:34–35

*D*ear Lord, as we read the Bible together, we begin to see how important it is to love each other. You ask us to, encourage us to, and even command us to do just that. Give us wisdom and grace to fulfill Your commandments, for then we will truly be Your disciples. Amen.

Loving Service

*Do not use your freedom to indulge the sinful nature;
rather, serve one another in love.*
GALATIANS 5:13

*P*recious Lord, You have given us a magnificent gift—one that You reserved for us alone. We have the freedom to make our own choices. Our old sinful nature wants to turn us inward, demanding that others meet our needs. But Your love urges us to turn outward, pouring out our love and service on others. Show us how to better serve You, each other, and everyone around us. Amen.

Putting Love First

Christ's love has moved me to such extremes.
His love has the first and last word in everything we do.
2 CORINTHIANS 5:14 MSG

*H*eavenly Father, we both want that last word, especially when we disagree and are both thinking of ourselves. We know we have to make peace if we are sincere in wanting to show love. No matter the issue, no matter the situation, we ask You to help us put love first. Amen.

First Priority

If I give all I possess to the poor and surrender my body to the flames,
but have not love, I gain nothing.
1 CORINTHIANS 13:3

*D*ear Father, so many things are vying for our attention—the children, the bills, our interests and ambitions. We know You want us to be successful in those things You have called us to do in life, but help us never forget that love is our first priority and first responsibility. Amen.

Loving as God Loves

Love is patient and kind. Love is not jealous, it does not brag, and it is not proud. Love is not rude, is not selfish, and does not get upset with others. Love does not count up wrongs that have been done.
1 CORINTHIANS 13:4–5 NCV

*D*ear Lord, You love us with a selfless, unconditional love—the highest height of love. We know that in the natural world we aren't capable of loving as You love, but we ask that Your Holy Spirit would help us love as purely and selflessly as possible. Amen.

A Prayer for the Help of the Holy Spirit

The fruit of the Spirit is love, joy, peace, patience, kindness, goodness, faithfulness.
GALATIANS 5:22

*D*ear Father, we know we are unable to love as we should without the help of Your Holy Spirit. We ask You now to dwell actively in our hearts and lives, showing us the ways of love and helping us to love with the purity that would otherwise be impossible for us. Thank You, Lord, for sending us Your Helper, the precious Spirit of God. Amen.

A Prayer for Encouragement

*Let us consider how we may spur one
another on toward love and good deeds.*
HEBREWS 10:24

*F*ather God, You have called us to live this life together in Your name. Remind us each day to speak words of encouragement and love to each other, words that would draw out the best virtues and the most noble deeds love has to offer. Thank You, Father, for showing us how to love You, each other, and those around us much better. Amen.

Our Commitment

The Power of Permanence

Never let loyalty and kindness leave you!
PROVERBS 3:3 NLT

*I*magine feeding your family dinner on the same old paper plates day after day. No matter how carefully you treat them, they were made to be disposable. They won't last. In fact, even the best paper plates won't withstand more than one meal before they're soiled, limp, and useless.

Unlike cheap paper plates, fine china plates were made to last. They are even considered heirlooms in many families, handed down from generation to generation. No trash can necessary. But just because china was designed to last doesn't mean it will. It must be handled carefully and stacked gently. It may even need to be washed by hand instead of in the dishwasher. It takes more than simply acquiring fine china to ensure it will be around to beautify the family table for years to come. A commitment must be made by those who own and use it—a commitment to handle it with great care.

When God designed marriage, He designed it to last. When something is permanent (at least in terms of life here on earth) it often bears wonderful qualities like strength, stability, and dependability. But for a marriage to last from the wedding day to the final day when a spouse meets Jesus face-to-face takes more than God's perfect design. It takes commitment from the husband and wife—commitment not just to stay together but to care for one another.

Marriage is certainly more precious and priceless than fine china, but it's often treated more like a paper plate: handy to have around, but readily disposable if something better comes along. How a husband and wife view the permanence of their marriage will make a difference in how they treat each other—and how long their relationship will last.

If a commitment to permanence goes hand in hand with a commitment to proper care, what "care instructions" are necessary for maintaining a marriage? The book of Proverbs is just one of the many guidebooks in scripture that provide sound advice for married couples. Wise words like, "Enjoy the wife you married as a young man! Lovely as an angel, beautiful as a rose—don't ever quit taking delight in her body. Never take her love for granted!" (Proverbs 5:18–19, MSG) can inspire both husbands and wives toward commitment and tender care that can last a lifetime. Why not read and pray your way through Proverbs as a couple this month? See what God has to teach you about caring for each other like fine china. Your example of loving commitment may become an heirloom that can be passed down through your family for generations to come.

Willing Hearts

If you make a promise to God, don't be slow to keep it. . .
give God what you promised.
ECCLESIASTES 5:4 NCV

*P*recious Father, we have made vows to each other and to You. Perhaps the reason You ask us to do that is because You know life is filled with ups and downs. Some days we are madly in love and can't get enough of each other; other days our egos get bruised or our feelings get hurt and everything changes. Give us the willingness to keep our promises in good times as well as in bad. Amen.

Committed Hearts

"Your hearts must be fully committed to the LORD our God,
to live by his decrees and obey his commands, as at this time."
1 KINGS 8:61

*H*eavenly Father, we believe that all Your commands were given to help us live happy and fulfilling lives—especially Your commands about marriage. Give us hearts that are fully committed to obeying, for we know that is our best path to a successful marriage. Amen.

God's Glorious Favor

*"I will look on you with favor and make you fruitful and increase
your numbers, and I will keep my covenant with you."*
LEVITICUS 26:9

*D*ear Lord, You are so awesome! You ask us to be faithful, to keep
our promises, and to remain committed in our relationship with
one another, and You give Your commands credibility by always
remaining faithful, committed, and true to Your Word. When
we follow Your example, You bless us even more by pouring out
Your favor on us. We don't know how to thank You enough for
all that You have done. Amen.

Loyal Hearts

*Many proclaim themselves loyal,
but who can find one worthy of trust?*
PROVERBS 20:6 NRSV

*O*ur Lord, we would never betray each other, but there are so
many little things we do or think that exhibit a lapse in our
loyalty to You and to each other. Show us where we need to
shore up our hearts and minds so we might be completely loyal
marriage partners. Amen.

Winning the Race

Let us run with endurance the race that is set before us.
HEBREWS 12:1 NKJV

*D*ear Father, it seems as though marriage is like a marathon. It's easy in the beginning, but as time passes, our lack of endurance begins to show, and we lose our steady pace. Our loving feelings start to fall behind the other thoughts and concerns in our lives, and we grow tired and defeated. Help us to stay the course and keep our love strong, so we can look back at the end of our lives and know that we won the race together. Amen.

Just and Faithful

Commit your way to the Lord; trust in him and he will do this: He will make your righteousness shine like the dawn, the justice of your cause like the noonday sun.
PSALM 37:5–6

*F*ather in heaven, our commitment to You has been strengthened by Your devoted commitment to us. You have taught us by Your example. Once again, we give You our lives and everything that concerns us. We know that all we are and all we hope to be is safe in Your arms. Thank You for Your just and faithful ways. Amen.

Leaving Our Requests

Commit everything you do to the Lord.
Trust him, and he will help you.
PSALM 37:5 NLT

*F*ather, we need Your help today as never before. We bring our requests and petitions before You. Thank You, Lord, for always making Your help available to us. We don't have to beg or go away wondering. We leave ourselves and our requests in Your hands, knowing that You will respond according to Your wisdom and power. Amen.

Holding Fast

Test everything. Hold on to the good. Avoid every kind of evil.
1 THESSALONIANS 5:21–22

*L*oving Father, there are so many traps along our marriage journey. Help us to avoid all the evil ploys to pull us away from each other. You've given us something good, and we desire to hold on to it. Help us remember that commitments are more often broken by carelessness than intention. We trust in You. Amen.

Due Season

*Let us not be weary in well doing:
for in due season we shall reap, if we faint not.*
GALATIANS 6:9 KJV

*L*ord, on those days when we feel like giving up on life and on each other, we ask for Your strength. Our own strength, as we have found, is just not enough. Even though we love each other and want to keep our commitment to one another, we quickly flounder when trouble and misunderstandings come. We look to You to renew our strength from Your bountiful supply. Amen.

Our Defender and Inspiration

The Spirit produces the fruit of. . .faithfulness.
GALATIANS 5:22 NCV

*H*oly Father, thank You for sending Your Holy Spirit to aid us as we work to faithfully keep our commitments to You and our marriage. Without Him, we would have no power or strength. The world would quickly crush everything good in our lives. Your Spirit is our defender and inspiration. Amen.

Love and Faithfulness

Let love and faithfulness never leave you; bind them around your neck, write them on the tablet of your heart. Then you will win favor and a good name in the sight of God and man.
PROVERBS 3:3–4

*D*ear Lord, You have taught us that what is in our hearts will determine what we do. Therefore, we ask that You help us bind love and faithfulness to our hearts, where it will grow and thrive and lead to behaviors in our relationship that are pleasing to You. Amen.

Being Trustworthy

It is required that those who have been given a trust must prove faithful.
1 CORINTHIANS 4:2

Lord God, we have placed our trust in You first and foremost. We long to be faithful to You. Chasten us when we lose faith or do things that are not pleasing to You. We know that fulfilling our commitment to You is the best way we can be faithful to one another. Amen.

A Sense of Permanence

*[Jesus said,] "Be faithful until death,
and I will give you the crown of life."*
REVELATION 2:10 NKJV

Heavenly Father, we look at the years ahead and wonder how we can stay strong in our marriage. There are so many obstacles and so many opportunities that could cause us to lose all You have given us. Give us endurance, Lord, a sense of permanence, and a love that will last a lifetime. Amen.

Follow-Through

Lord, who may dwell in your sanctuary?
Who may live on your holy hill? . . .
[He] who keeps his oath even when it hurts. . .
PSALM 15:1, 4

*F*ather, we made a promise to love, honor, and cherish You and each other on our wedding day. That sounded very easy in the beginning, but over time we have encountered obstacles that have made us feel like giving up. Thank You for giving us the stamina to keep holding on even when we want to do just the opposite. You are the strength of our lives together. Amen.

Our Family

The Power of Flesh and Blood

*I bow my knees before the Father, from whom every
family in heaven and on earth takes its name.*
EPHESIANS 3:14–15 NRSV

*F*amilies were God's idea. Way back in the beginning (as described in the first two chapters of Genesis), God drew men and women together like two perfectly matched puzzle pieces. As "bone of my bones and flesh of my flesh," God fused two into one in a miraculous way. Family was the result.

Not every family will have biological children, but every husband and wife can enjoy the blessing of spiritual children, those individuals God brings across your path for you to love and mentor and encourage in their faith in God. Spiritual children can be any age, and they may or may not be related to you in a natural sense. They are children in that have not yet come to maturity in their walk with God and would benefit from the presence of those who are older and more experienced in spiritual matters. Whether a family includes biological, adopted, step, or spiritual children, every child can use the support of a praying parent—and every parent can learn a lesson in supportive prayer from Hannah.

In 1 Samuel 1, we are introduced to a woman named Hannah, who dearly longed to have a child. But year after year, her desire remained unfulfilled. In desperation, she offered a tearful prayer, promising to dedicate her child fully to God if He would allow her the blessing of motherhood. Her prayer was answered with the birth of Samuel, whose name means, "heard of God."

After Samuel was weaned, Hannah took her only son to the home of Eli the priest. In 1 Samuel 1:27–28 she explains to Eli, "I prayed for this child, and the Lord has granted me what I asked of him. So now I give him to the Lord." Hannah fulfilled her vow by leaving her son in Eli's care. As the years passed, Samuel grew up to be one of the celebrated prophets of the Old Testament.

Today, few parents dedicate their children to God by leaving them in the care of the church. But that doesn't mean dedicating children to God is obsolete. Holding your children close to God in prayer is a powerful way to give them to the Lord like Hannah did. Not only do your prayers invite God to work miracles in your children's lives, but they serve as a reminder that your children's future ultimately lies in God's hands—not yours.

God has given you the privilege and responsibility of caring for your children for the duration of their lives on earth, but He will be the Father who cares for them throughout eternity. God's design for family extends further than the reaches of this life. Although marriage and childbirth will come to an earthly end, the relationship of parent and child, husband and wife, brother and sister, will not. Family will be redefined in paradise. But until then, you can work hand in hand with God through prayer, supporting your family, and guiding each member on their personal journey to Christ.

Proud and Happy

"I will receive you. I will be a Father to you,
and you will be my sons and daughters," says the Lord Almighty.
2 CORINTHIANS 6:17–18

*D*ear Lord, thank You for receiving us into Your family and acknowledging us as Your own son and daughter. We know You will always be there to help us and take care of us, just as we love and care for our children. We are proud and happy to be Your children. Amen.

A Prayer for Truth

I have no greater joy than this, to hear that
my children are walking in the truth.
3 JOHN 1:4 NRSV

*D*ear Father, You are the author of truth, and we know there is no deceit in You at all. We want to walk in the truth because we know that is how we can always be in Your presence. We pray also for our children. Help us to set an example for our children and teach them to recognize and follow the truth. Amen.

Fatherly Restraint

Fathers, provoke not your children to wrath: but bring
them up in the nurture and admonition of the Lord.
EPHESIANS 6:4 KJV

*H*eavenly Father, I am so imperfect and often react without thinking, especially when I've had a long and frustrating day. But Lord, I want to be the kind of father to my children that You are to me—the kind that can be trusted to show loving discipline and restraint. Thank You, Lord, for helping me approach my children with wisdom and love. Amen.

Motherly Strength

A wise woman strengthens her family.
PROVERBS 14:1 NCV

*F*ather God, I want to be the kind of woman who brings strength and encouragement to my family; the kind that shows love in all situations; the kind that is pleasing to You. I ask for the wisdom to lovingly manage my family. Remind me to listen to Your voice and avoid stressful distractions and fatigue. I look to You to make me the kind of mother my children and my husband can place their trust in. Amen.

We Are Part of God's Family

You are no longer strangers and aliens, but you are citizens
with the saints and also members of the household of God,
built upon the foundation of the apostles and prophets,
with Christ Jesus himself as the cornerstone.
EPHESIANS 2:19–20 NRSV

*L*ord God, thank You for making us part of Your family. We are excited to be included in the same household as the great men and women of faith throughout the ages! Enter into our lives, Lord, and remain the center of our marriage, home, and family all our days. Amen.

Sacrificial Love

[Jesus said to his disciples,] "Whoever wishes to become great among
you must be your servant, and whoever wishes to be first among you
must be slave of all. For the Son of Man came not to be served but to
serve, and to give his life a ransom for many."
MARK 10:43–45 NRSV

*L*ord Jesus, we pray for You to take away the selfishness in our hearts and replace it with a servant's attitude. Let us honor You by cultivating an attitude of godly sacrifice for the benefit of our spouse, our family, and our community. Amen.

Raising Godly Children

*The father of a good child is very happy; parents who have
wise children are glad because of them. Make your father
and mother happy; give your mother a reason to be glad.*
PROVERBS 23:24–25 NCV

*F*ather God, we pray for our children, knowing that we are
powerless to raise them properly without Your help. Help us to
instill wisdom in their hearts so that they will have the tools to
make good choices and live in a way that brings happiness and
joy to our hearts. Amen.

Wise Training

Train children in the right way, and when old, they will not stray.
PROVERBS 22:6 NRSV

*L*ord God, give us the wisdom and courage to raise our children
with strong, godly values. Help us to turn a deaf ear to the world
and those who would point opposite the principles in Your
Word, the Bible. Give us the strength to stick to our guns and
raise our children to love and obey You. Amen.

Undeserved Gifts

Children are a gift from the Lord;
they are a reward from him.
PSALM 127:3 NLT

*F*ather God, how can we thank You for the children You have given us? We are in awe of such wonderful, undeserved gifts. Teach us how to be worthy of Your trust in us as parents, and remind us always that our children are our most precious gift from You. Amen.

A Godly Family

It takes wisdom to have a good family,
and it takes understanding to make it strong.
PROVERBS 24:3 NCV

*H*oly Father, we ask for the wisdom and understanding necessary to raise our children and direct the affairs of our lives in a way that is pleasing to You. Show us as a family how to live together in harmony and how to honor one another as we continue to honor You as the most important member of our family. Amen.

A Prayer with a Promise

Keep [God's] decrees and commands, which I am giving you today, so that it may go well with you and your children after you and that you may live long in the land the LORD your God gives you for all time.
DEUTERONOMY 4:40

*F*ather God, Your Word, the Bible, tells us how to live godly lives in this world. We ask You to help us strive to obey Your commands and raise our children to do the same. Thank You for Your promise to prosper us and give us a long and happy life together. Amen.

Peace for the Children

All thy children shall be taught of the Lord;
and great shall be the peace of thy children.
ISAIAH 54:13 KJV

*D*ear Lord, we want to give our children the advantage of being taught from Your Word. Remind us to keep up on daily readings of Your Word and to continually seek out Your ways through the Holy Spirit. We know this will give us the tools we need to pass Your wisdom and understanding on to our children. We will surely praise You all over again when we see our children living in peace and prosperity. Amen.

The Family of Believers

*As we have opportunity, let us do good to all people,
especially to those who belong to the family of believers.*
GALATIANS 6:10

*H*oly Father, our family is a large one that extends to all those
who love You and have been adopted into Your body of believers.
Nudge us when there is an opportunity to help one of our
spiritual brothers or sisters. We consider it an honor to give back
what You have given us. Amen.

Family Service

"As for me and my family, we will serve the LORD."
JOSHUA 24:15 NCV

*F*ather God, open our hearts to see the multitude of opportunities around us to serve You by serving others. Show us the
brokenhearted, the poor, the disadvantaged, and the fearful.
Lead us to those who lack understanding so that we might point
them to You, their heavenly Father. Amen.

Our Home

The Power of Refuge and Refreshment

My people will live in peaceful dwelling places,
in secure homes, in undisturbed places of rest.
ISAIAH 32:18

*H*ome is more than an address. For a husband and wife, it's where the masks come off, the defenses come down, and the complexities of learning to love others unconditionally are revealed. Home can be a place of refuge and refreshment or tension and resentment. Much of that distinction depends on who is deemed the head of the household.

When God is the true head of a home, prayer becomes a language that is spoken naturally and freely within its halls. And when spouses pray regularly for one another, they will find their hearts becoming more tender toward each other. They will be more willing to listen, learn, and forgive. Power struggles over who is right and who has the final word will transform into peaceful resolutions as God teaches both husband and wife what it means to love others as they love themselves.

Change does not happen overnight, but when God is the head of a home, change does take place. As husbands and wives mature in their love for each other, that love will change the atmosphere of their home. Their home will become an inviting safe haven for all those who enter its doors—family, friends, and strangers alike.

Your home can be a sanctuary to others: a place of joy, hope, and retreat—a refuge permeated with prayer. Opening the doors of your home like this may feel a bit risky. And it is. Love always involves risk. But being hospitable doesn't require anything more than love. It doesn't require gourmet meals or designer decor. Simply open your door and your heart with a willingness to share what God has so freely shared with you. You just might find that you are the one who ends up feeling blessed.

Pray together for each and every person who enters your home, and you will see miracles happen before your eyes. Hearts will be changed, loads will be lifted, and brokenness will be healed. Most importantly, God will be glorified in your midst. When your home is a place of blessing for all who pay a visit, imagine what it would be like for those who live there: God's love and care unlimited!

A Prayer of Thanks for Refuge

*In the fear of the Lord one has strong confidence,
and one's children will have a refuge.*
PROVERBS 14:26 NRSV

*H*eavenly Father, we live in a dangerous world. Thank You for helping us make our home a place of refuge for our family. Fill each room with Your presence, we pray, bringing warmth and new life to what would otherwise be an intricate arrangement of wood, brick, and plaster. You are an awesome God! Amen.

Laughter at Home

*A cheerful look brings joy to the heart,
and good news gives health to the bones.*
PROVERBS 15:30

*F*ather in heaven, make our home a place of laughter. We know the simple joy that laughter brings comes straight from You. Thank You for making it an essential part of our lives, bringing us a healthy perspective on the things we encounter each day. Amen.

A Prayer of Thanks for Protection

*"Have you not put a hedge around him and his household and
everything he has? You have blessed the work of his hands,
so that his flocks and herds are spread throughout the land."*
Job 1:10

*D*ear Father, not only have You made our home a shining
beacon in this world, but You have promised to send Your angels
to protect and care for us. What great thanks we owe You for all
the relaxation and security You have provided. Thank You for all
Your goodness. Amen.

God's Blessing on Our Home

*All you who fear GOD, how blessed you are! . . .
Revel in the goodness! Your wife will bear children as a vine bears grapes,
your household lush as a vineyard, the children around your
table as fresh and promising as young olive shoots.*
Psalm 128:1–4 MSG

*G*ood Father, each day we feel Your presence here. Your blessings
surround us. We don't deserve all the goodness that You pour out
on us, but we are pleased to receive it because of all Your precious
Son endured to guarantee it. We are so grateful! Amen.

Agreement in Prayer

*When any two of you on earth agree about something you are praying
for, my Father in heaven will do it for you. Whenever two or three
of you come together in my name, I am there with you.*
MATTHEW 18:19–20 CEV

*L*ord Jesus, how wonderful is Your promise to be with us
whenever we gather together. Make our home a place where we
can assemble as family and friends in Your name. For when we
come together for Your purposes, Your power and presence is
multiplied. Thank You, Lord, for reminding us that we need
each other. Amen.

A Prayer of Consecration

*You shall love the Lord your God with all your heart,
and with all your soul, and with all your might.*
DEUTERONOMY 6:5 NRSV

*D*ear Lord, everything we have has come from You, and we grant
You full control over every of space in this home, all it contains,
and all those who live within these walls. Everything is Yours,
Lord. Give us Your wisdom as we attempt to raise our children in
loving submission to You and Your perfect will. Amen.

A Godly Reign

*Tell the older men to be temperate, serious, prudent,
and sound in faith, in love, and in endurance. Likewise,
tell the older women. . .they are to teach what is good.*
TITUS 2:2–3 NRSV

*F*ather, each day we feel Your presence admonishing, forgiving, and maturing us. We are glad to be molded into the kind of people who are pleasing in Your sight. We ask that those who enter here will sense, without judgment, that godliness reigns in this home. May we have a godly atmosphere characterized by the joy of being Your children. Amen.

Walking Our Talk

*He will direct his children and his household after him to
keep the way of the LORD by doing what is right and just.*
GENESIS 18:19

*H*oly God, it's not always easy to walk our talk when we are in our home with close friends. Sometimes we let our guard down and do or say things that bring us shame. Admonish us when our actions are inconsistent with the principles of Your Word. Give us courage to do and say things that are pleasing to You. May our words and actions reflect the holiness You bring to our home. Amen.

Coming Together

All the believers were together. . . .
They broke bread in their homes and ate
together with glad and sincere hearts.
ACTS 2:44, 46

*H*oly Father, the earliest Christians didn't have fancy churches to meet in; their homes were where they met to learn about You, enjoy fellowship with other believers, and worship You. Help us make our home a place of worship as well, a holy place where You are always welcome. Amen.

Reaching Out

*Cheerfully share your home with those
who need a meal or a place to stay.*
1 PETER 4:9 NLT

*H*eavenly Father, we pray for those who are hurting today, those who are in need of food and shelter. Show us how to reach out to those in need. We know we must be wise, but we are confident that You will show us those who truly need a helping hand. We promise to listen closely for Your voice. Amen.

Taking in Strangers

*Do not forget to entertain strangers. . . . Remember those
in prison as if you were their fellow prisoners, and those
who are mistreated as if you yourselves were suffering.*
HEBREWS 13:2–3

*L*ord God, we live in a dangerous world, a place where some strangers can pose a threat to us and our children. Still, we hear Your call to reach out to those You send our way. Give us the grace to reach out without fear, believing that You will warn us when danger is near. Thank You for the privilege of extending Your welcoming love. Amen.

Honoring God's Presence

Jesus replied, "If anyone loves me, he will obey my teaching. My Father will love him, and we will come to him and make our home with him."
JOHN 14:23

*F*ather God, thank You for Your promise to come and make Your home with us. We honor You both as master and revered guest of our home. May we keep ourselves fit and holy out of respect for the great privilege we have to welcome You into our hearts. Amen.

The Gift of Unity

Behold, how good and how pleasant it is
for brethren to dwell together in unity!
PSALM 133:1 KJV

*D*ear Lord, it is a glorious privilege to dwell together in joy and harmony with those we love. We owe our unity to Your presence in our home. Thank You for establishing us as an oasis of cool refreshment in a dry and thirsty world. Amen.

Sharing the Peace and Harmony

Share with God's people who are in need.
Practice hospitality.
ROMANS 12:13

*D*ear Lord, we know how greatly we've been blessed. Our home may be small by some standards, but it is filled with love. Show us how to open our home to others, sharing the peace and harmony that dwells here as a result of Your presence. Amen.

Our Calling

The Power of Living for God

Lead a life worthy of the calling to which you have
been called, with all humility and gentleness, with patience,
bearing with one another in love, making every effort to
maintain the unity of the Spirit in the bond of peace.
EPHESIANS 4:1–3 NRSV

*T*here are two possible responses to a ringing phone: answer it or ignore it. When God calls, we have those same options. There are, however, many people who wait for God's call, hear it, but remain uncertain if they actually heard a ring or not. They believe that God may be calling them, but they are so fearful of misunderstanding God's command that they go with option number two: They ignore what they think they may have heard and wait for a louder ring.

God's call can be specific. Scripture records how God called people to be prophets, kings, and apostles. However, much more frequently in scripture, God's call is given in more general terms. He calls His children to live in freedom (Galatians 5:13), to lead holy lives (1 Thessalonians 4:7; 2 Timothy 1:9), to live in peace (1 Corinthians 7:15), to walk in God's light instead of darkness (1 Peter 2:9–10), and to live a life worthy of God's call to salvation (Ephesians 4:1). These kinds of calls are easy to understand. Answering them is something else altogether.

71

Answering God's call to live out freedom, peace, and holiness in daily life requires more than just determination. It requires a continual refill of God's Spirit, wisdom, and strength. Husbands and wives can help each other answer this call by encouraging one another to live lives worthy of service in God's name.

God often calls husbands and wives to service together. The possibilities are limitless: pastoral work, counseling, music ministry, ministry to children, prayer, etc. Seek God together to learn what His special calling is for the two of you. You may be surprised at the increased blessings that come from serving God together.

If you and your spouse are unsure of what God's calling you to do at this time, make sure you are acting on what you already know God has asked of you. Then call out to God. Jeremiah 33:3 says, "Call to me and I will answer you and tell you great and unsearchable things you do not know." Scripture promises that God will always answer your call.

The High Calling

You are the ones chosen by God, chosen for the high calling
of priestly work, chosen to be a holy people, God's instruments
to do his work and speak out for him, to tell others of
the night-and-day difference he made for you.
1 PETER 2:9–10 MSG

*H*eavenly Father, what a privilege and honor it is to know that You have called us to be part of Your kingdom. We say "yes" to whatever You have planned for us. Begin to open our hearts and minds in preparation for Your calling. Amen.

Identifying God's Calling

It was [God] who gave some to be apostles, some to be prophets, some to
be evangelists, and some to be pastors and teachers. . .so that the body of
Christ may be built up until we all reach unity in the faith.
EPHESIANS 4:11–13

*D*ear Lord, help us as we endeavor to identify the specific gifts and callings that are ever-present in our lives. Only You truly know who we really are and what we have been called to do. Show us as we submit ourselves to You and Your perfect will. Amen.

Boldness in God's Calling

God doesn't want us to be shy with his gifts,
but bold and loving and sensible.
2 TIMOTHY 1:7 MSG

*D*ear Father, we are eager to see what You have in store for us individually and as a couple. As You reveal what You have placed within us, show us how to boldly put those gifts to work for the sake of Your kingdom. Amen.

Confidence in God's Calling

If anyone speaks, he should do it as one speaking the very words of God.
If anyone serves, he should do it with the strength God provides,
so that in all things God may be praised through Jesus Christ.
1 PETER 4:11

*D*ear Lord, give us the confidence we need to overcome whatever obstacles stand in the way of the calling You have determined for us. Whatever it is, we want to do it with all our might so that You will be praised in heaven and on earth. Amen.

Wholehearted Service

Serve wholeheartedly, as if you were serving the Lord, not men, because you know that the Lord will reward everyone for whatever good he does.
EPHESIANS 6:7–8

*H*oly God, to serve You is a privilege and an honor no matter what You have called us to do. We ask for the endurance and faith to serve You without doubt, without reservation, and with nothing held back. We want to pursue our calling in a way that allows us to reach our full potential in You. Amen.

Sacrificial Service

"The King will reply, 'I tell you the truth, whatever you did for one of the least of these brothers of mine, you did for me.' "
MATTHEW 25:40

*H*eavenly Father, You have given us so much. What else could we do but serve You with all our hearts? We know that putting Your kingdom first will cost us, but we also know that anything we do for the least of Your children is the highest service we could possibly undertake. We love You, Lord. Amen.

Performing Our Duties

*Keep your head in all situations,
endure hardship, do the work of an evangelist,
discharge all the duties of your ministry.*
2 TIMOTHY 4:5

*L*ord God, You haven't called us just to sit and watch. You've called us to get involved and actively pursue the duties associated with the calling You've placed on our lives. We pledge to put one foot in front of the other and take it slow—always doing our best to follow the path You have set before us. Thank You for trusting us to be part of Your mighty purpose and plan. Amen.

A Prayer for Competence

Such confidence as this is ours through Christ before God.
Not that we are competent in ourselves to claim anything for ourselves,
but our competence comes from God.
2 CORINTHIANS 3:4–5

*H*oly Father, You know that we are nothing by ourselves. We must have Your help and guidance as we pursue our great calling. Give us wisdom and counsel, courage and confidence, as we move forward to follow You into unknown waters. We promise to do our best and trust You no matter what. Amen.

A Prayer for Reconciliation

God was reconciling the world to himself in Christ, not counting
men's sins against them. And he has committed to us the message
of reconciliation. We are therefore Christ's ambassadors,
as though God were making his appeal through us.
2 CORINTHIANS 5:19–20

*F*ather, all Christians are called to take Your message of love and reconciliation to the world. We want to be worthy ambassadors of Your Word. We pray that You would help us recognize the opportunities that come our way to serve as ambassadors for You and Your kingdom. Amen.

A Prayer for Bearing Fruit

We pray this in order that you may live a life worthy of the Lord and may please him in every way: bearing fruit in every good work.
COLOSSIANS 1:10

Holy Father, it is our greatest desire to please You in every aspect of our lives. Pursuing Your call means nothing if we are not living lives worthy of that call. As we commit to consistent prayer and study of Your Word, we pray that we would bear fruit—the fruit of love, patience, kindness, joy, peace, goodness, faithfulness, gentleness, and self-control. Amen.

Spreading the Good News

How beautiful on the mountains are the feet of those who bring good news, who proclaim peace, who bring good tidings, who proclaim salvation, who say to Zion, "Your God reigns!"
ISAIAH 52:7

Lord God, we marvel at Your salvation. We feel deeply the call to spread the Good News to all we come in contact with. Thank You, Lord, for giving us the words to speak when we need them—words that will win hearts over to Your kingdom. Amen.

Sacrifice for the Sake of the Good News

[Jesus said,] "If you try to hang on to your life,
you will lose it. But if you give up your life for my sake
and for the sake of the Good News, you will save it."
MARK 8:35 NLT

*H*eavenly Father, giving of ourselves to share the Good News will sometimes mean sacrificing our time, energy, and money. There will be times when we will need to set aside our desires and livelihoods in order to ensure that others might know You and live. Give us the grace to follow Your example of sacrificial living. Amen.

Sanctified Service

In your hearts sanctify Christ as Lord. Always be ready to
make your defense to anyone who demands from you
an accounting for the hope that is in you.
1 PETER 3:15 NRSV

*H*oly Father, our efforts and sacrifices to fulfill our calling on behalf of the Good News of the gospel will be of no avail if we do not keep our hearts clean and holy before You. Wash us clean, Lord. When we speak in defense of our faith, we pray that our words will flow freely from hearts made righteous by You. Amen.

The Ultimate Calling

"Go therefore and make disciples of all nations, baptizing them in
the name of the Father and of the Son and of the Holy Spirit, and
teaching them to obey everything that I have commanded you."
MATTHEW 28:19–20 NRSV

*D*ear Lord, there is no greater calling than to be Your disciple. That is what we want to be more than anything. Show us how to listen to Your voice and quickly obey Your commands. We promise to follow where You lead. Give us opportunities to show others how to become disciples as well. Amen.

Our Gifts

The Power of Faithful Service

Every desirable and beneficial gift comes out of heaven.
The gifts are rivers of light cascading down from the Father of Light.
JAMES 1:16 MSG

*I*magine choosing a very special gift for someone. The person acts excited upon receiving the gift, comments on the beautiful wrapping paper, shakes the box to try and guess what's inside, offers a word of thanks, and then sets the gift on a shelf. There it will sit, unopened, gathering dust year after year.

Now imagine that the giver of this wonderful gift is God. Scripture paints a picture of God as a thoughtful, gracious, and faithful giver. A loving Father does not give His children cheap little trinkets they can't use or shouldn't want. He gives them useful things they need; He gives them carefully chosen treasures meant to be opened and enjoyed.

The gifts God gives are plentiful and varied. They include the miracles of life, love, and salvation, as well as daily provisions like food, shelter, and clothing. But there is one category of gifts God chooses with special care for each of His children: spiritual gifts. These gifts are unique in that they are designed to be used for the benefit of others.

1 Corinthians 12:4–7 says, "There are different kinds of spiritual gifts, but the same Spirit is the source of them all. There are different kinds of service, but we serve the same

Lord. God works in different ways, but it is the same God who does the work in all of us. A spiritual gift is given to each of us so we can help each other" (NLT). Spiritual gifts can include teaching, providing wise counsel, and leading people to a personal relationship with God.

It's true that the "wrapping" of some spiritual gifts may draw more attention than others. For example, preaching a sermon is a much more public gift than stuffing inserts into the church bulletin. A musical gift may be more glamorous than the gift of caring for the sick or elderly. However, no gift is more important or useful than another, and every gift is bestowed on just the right person. Be confident in the gifts God has chosen for you, and encourage the members of your family to use theirs to the best of their ability.

If you are unsure of what spiritual gift God has given you, ask Him to help you unwrap it and understand how you can share that gift generously to benefit others.

A Prayer of Thanks for God's Gifts

*"You did not choose me but I chose you. And I appointed you
to go and bear fruit, fruit that will last, so that the Father
will give you whatever you ask him in my name."*
JOHN 15:16 NRSV

*D*ear Lord, mere words are not enough to properly thank You for all the wonderful things You have brought to our lives. On top of Your forgiveness, salvation, and remarkable love, You have given us special gifts to help us share our faith with others. Help us as we endeavor to use our gifts for Your glory and praise. Amen.

A Prayer of Thanks for God's Grace

*We all have different gifts, each of which
came because of the grace God gave us.*
ROMANS 12:6 NCV

*G*lorious Father, You could have made us all alike—little clones of Yourself—following orders from now until eternity. But You chose to do something else—something remarkably daring and creative. You made us all unique, endowed us with free will, and gave us different gifts to help make Your glory known throughout the world. We are in awe of You, sweet Lord. Amen.

A Prayer of Thanks for Useful Gifts

Each one should use whatever gift he has received to serve others,
faithfully administering God's grace in its various forms. . .
so that in all things God may be praised through Jesus Christ.
1 PETER 4:10–11

*H*eavenly Father, sometimes we're given gifts that seem useless, but Your gifts are always given with a purpose in mind. Help us to identify our gifts and show us how to use them in an exciting and productive way. Amen.

A Prayer of Thanks for Irrevocable Gifts

God's gifts and his call can never be withdrawn.
ROMANS 11:29 NLT

*S*weet Father, You must look down on us and wonder if You have given us our gifts in vain, if we are ever going to understand how they were meant to be used. However, You do not snatch them away in frustration. Instead, You gently lead us toward their purpose. Help us live up to Your expectations of us and bring You praise. Amen.

A Prayer of Thanks for General Gifts

To the man who pleases him,
God gives wisdom, knowledge and happiness.
ECCLESIASTES 2:26

*F*ather God, some of Your gifts are unique and specialized, but others are there for the taking. You have promised all of us wisdom if we are willing to receive it, knowledge if we are willing to pursue it, and happiness if we are willing to embrace it. Thank You for all Your gifts. Amen.

A Prayer of Thanks for Creative Gifts

I have filled [you] with the Spirit of God, with skill,
ability and knowledge in all kinds of crafts.
EXODUS 31:3

*H*eavenly Father, You are the great Creator who made heaven and earth and all that we see around us. We are so blessed that You have endowed us with creativity as well. Because of this generous gift, we can express ourselves in an infinite variety of ways. Show us how to go about encouraging that creativity in each other. Amen.

A Prayer of Thanks for the Gift-Giver

*There are different kinds of spiritual gifts, but the same
Spirit is the source of them all. There are different kinds of service,
but the same Lord we serve. God works in different ways,
but it is the same God who does the work in all of us.*
1 CORINTHIANS 12:4–6 NLT

*H*oly Father, Your Word reminds us that Your Spirit is the source of all the gifts You've bestowed upon Your believers. What an honor it is to be commissioned by You and to work side by side with others as You give us direction. Amen.

A Prayer of Thanks for God's Greatest Gift

*[Jesus said,] "If you then, though you are evil, know how to
give good gifts to your children, how much more will your Father
in heaven give the Holy Spirit to those who ask him!"*
LUKE 11:13

*L*ord God, we recognize that Your Holy Spirit is the greatest gift we could possibly receive. We can hardly believe that You have sent Your Spirit to live in our hearts and help us live in a way that is pleasing to You. Help us to listen carefully as You teach us how to use our gifts for Your honor and glory. Amen.

A Prayer of Thanks for the Blessing of Gifts

*In [God] you have been enriched in every way —
in all your speaking and in all your knowledge.*
1 CORINTHIANS 1:5

Lord God, we are very aware that the gifts You've placed in our lives are meant to benefit others and bring glory and honor to Your name, but they also make our own lives more fulfilling and expressive. It's as though the vessel is better for having held the water. We thank You for the opportunity to use Your gifts. Amen.

A Prayer of Anointing

"You did not choose me, but I chose you and appointed you to go and bear fruit—fruit that will last. Then the Father will give you whatever you ask in my name."
JOHN 15:16

*F*ather God, it is a great honor to know that You have chosen each of us to take Your gifts and use them to spread a greater understanding of who You are to others and what You have done for them. Thank You for choosing us. We believe that You have anointed us to carry out Your assignments. Amen.

A Prayer of Constancy

Do not neglect the spiritual gift you received through the prophecy spoken over you when the elders of the church laid their hands on you.
1 TIMOTHY 4:14 NLT

*F*ather God, this world can be an exhausting place to live, and we know that the enthusiasm we feel right now may not always last. We ask that Your Holy Spirit would continue to inspire and motivate us as the months and years go by, and that we would always use our gifts as they were intended and never neglect them. Amen.

A Prayer for Inspiration

*I remind you to fan into flames the spiritual
gift God gave you when I laid my hands on you.*
2 TIMOTHY 1:6 NLT

*L*ord God, as You inspire us to carry on Your work, using the gifts You have bestowed, show us how to keep the flames of passion and excitement for our mission ignited in our hearts. We promise to come to You when the world seems to overwhelm us. Inspire us anew to do Your work day after day. Amen.

A Prayer of Purpose

*If a man's gift is. . .serving, let him serve; if it is teaching, let him teach;
if it is encouraging, let him encourage; if it is contributing to the needs
of others, let him give generously; if it is leadership, let him govern
diligently; if it is showing mercy, let him do it cheerfully.*
ROMANS 12:6–8

*H*oly God, help us as we identify how to effectively use the gifts You have given us. Stop us short if we begin to take Your gifts for granted. Remind us often of their power in our lives and others'. Amen.

A Prayer of Thanks for the Power of Gifts

A gift opens the way for the giver and ushers him into the presence of the great.
PROVERBS 18:16

*D*ear Lord, Your gifts are marvelous and astonishingly powerful. They provide endless opportunities by unexpectedly opening the way before us. Help us go eagerly wherever Your gifts may take us, and give us the courage to speak Your name with confidence and zeal. Amen.

Our Goals

The Power of Purpose

Our only goal is to please God.
2 CORINTHIANS 5:9 NCV

*D*avid was a man of God with an admirable goal: He wanted to build a permanent home for God. The ark of the covenant, where God allowed His presence to dwell, had been carried through the desert by the Israelites, captured by the Philistines, forgotten for twenty years, and then brought triumphantly into Jerusalem during David's reign. Though David made building plans for a great temple and even started collecting construction materials, it was his son, Solomon, who actually reached his father's goal. Solomon is the king who is best remembered for constructing the original temple in Jerusalem.

Though David had a goal, he consulted God before attempting to carry it out. God made it clear He wanted a man of peace—not war—to build His house. In obedience, David passed his pet project down to his son. However, Solomon never could have completed such a massive project in a mere seven years without the help of his 100,000-plus laborers, stonecutters, craftsmen, and construction managers—and a lot of prayer.

Any goal—whether it's as grand as building a house for God or as mundane as balancing a household budget—is worthy of prayer. Proverbs 16:3 says, "Commit to the Lord whatever you do, and your plans will succeed." Plans committed to God succeed because their worth is first weighed at the foot of God's throne. Goals that are not in line with God's will and His ways should not be pursued beyond this first step.

But the power of prayer doesn't end there. The wisdom of Proverbs 16 continues in verse 9 with the reminder that "We can make our plans, but the Lord determines our steps" (NLT). Even after a goal is set, plans are accomplished one step at a time. In the same way that checking a compass every now and then keeps a hiker on the right path, regularly returning to God in prayer while working toward a goal will keep a project moving in the right direction.

As husband and wife, it's natural to discuss your hopes and dreams with each other. Even individual goals like losing weight or finding a new job are more likely to succeed when you talk them over with God and your spouse.

It's important to remember that much of the value in reaching your goals is in the journey rather than the victory celebration at the end. Throughout your life, you will be setting, working toward, and reaching a variety of important goals. Through that process, God will be infusing His character and virtues into your life. Each time you and your spouse achieve an individual or joint goal, be sure to give God the glory and thank Him for all you've accomplished along the way.

God's Goals

*"I know the plans I have for you," declares the LORD, "plans to prosper
you and not to harm you, plans to give you hope and a future."*
JEREMIAH 29:11

*D*ear Lord, Your assurance gives us the courage to plan for our
future with confidence. No matter what the days may bring,
Your intentions for us are always good and filled with purpose.
Remain with us as we plan and achieve godly goals, and grant us
the wisdom to accept Your will in all things. Amen.

The Gift of Productive Work

*Always give yourselves fully to the work of the Lord,
because you know that your labor in the Lord is not in vain.*
1 CORINTHIANS 15:58

*G*racious God, thank You for the special gifts, talents, and skills
each of us possesses. Though these things may differ from person
to person, teach us to use our unique gifts in faithful service to
one another, ever appreciating and respecting the work and role
of our spouse. Amen.

Pressing Forward

*Forgetting those things which are behind and reaching forward
to those things which are ahead, I press toward the goal for
the prize of the upward call of God in Christ Jesus.*
PHILIPPIANS 3:13–14 NKJV

*D*ear Lord, throughout Your earthly life and ministry, You remained faithful to the goal of winning our salvation, even though it required a great deal of pain and suffering. Let us rely on Your strength and promise, especially when hindrances and hardships tempt us to abandon godly goals. Help us follow Your example so we may press on with confidence toward eternal life in You. Amen.

Relying on God's Power

*With God's power working in us, God can do much,
much more than anything we can ask or imagine.*
EPHESIANS 3:20 NCV

*A*lmighty Father, scripture tells us of Your ability and willingness to work great things in the lives of those who put their trust in You. So often though, we hesitate to bring You the true yearnings of our hearts, fearing perhaps that they are too big, too out of reach, too much to ask. But with You, nothing is impossible! Fill us with confidence in Your power to work great things in us and through us. Amen.

Faithful Endurance

*I don't care what happens to me, as long as I
finish the work that the Lord Jesus gave me to do.*
ACTS 20:24 CEV

*D*ear Lord Jesus, as You completed Your earthly work of sacrifice for our sake, let us complete the godly work You have graciously given us to do together. We pray that we will fully embrace the true nature of Your calling to serve each other and our family—especially when we're tempted to lessen our efforts. Grant us the endurance to face all things together with faith, compassion, patience, and fortitude. Amen.

Humbling Ourselves

*I do not mean that I am already as God wants me to be. I have not yet
reached that goal, but I continue trying to reach it and to make it mine.*
PHILIPPIANS 3:12 NCV

*L*ord God, You have given us the sacred gift of marriage to
cherish as husband and wife. We know we both fall short of the
people You would like us to be, but we humbly pray for Your
help and strength as we recommit ourselves to give more, serve
more, and love more. Amen.

A Runner's Heart

*Do you not know that in a race all the runners run,
but only one gets the prize? Run in such a way as to get the prize.*
1 CORINTHIANS 9:24

*D*ear Lord, through Your life, death, and resurrection, You have
won for us the prize we could never win for ourselves—salvation
and eternal life. In praise and thanksgiving, let us respond by
wholeheartedly applying ourselves to the race You have set before
us, with our eyes on the prize You have won for us. Amen.

Give Us a Singular Vision

*"Those who find their life will lose it, and those
who lose their life for my sake will find it."*
MATTHEW 10:39 NRSV

*H*eavenly Father, we both have ideas about the goals we want to
pursue in our lives. We ask though that You, knowing both our
hearts, will create in us a singular vision—a vision that conforms
to Your own plans for our lives and marriage. We know that we
will both be fulfilled in that vision, losing nothing of who we are
as individuals, but achieving all that You have called us to do.
Amen.

God's Good Purpose

*May He grant you according to your heart's desire,
and fulfill all your purpose.*
PSALM 20:4 NKJV

*G*iver of all good things, You know everything—even the deepest
desires of our hearts. Look with favor upon us as we bring these
desires before You, and guide us as we explore new opportunities,
plan our strategies, and work toward the goals we have set for
ourselves. Though all our days, let Your will be done and Your
purposes be fulfilled. Amen.

Seeking God's Help

If the Lord delights in a man's way, he makes his steps firm.
PSALM 37:23

Dear Lord God, You have promised to be with us always, strengthen us in every good work, and bless us with the gifts of Your Spirit. With confidence we come together to ask for Your continued help as we give our time and attention to the goals and plans we have made for the good of our marriage and family. As we journey, help us remain true to each other and true to You. Amen.

A Prayer for God's Strength

Job replied to the LORD: "I know that you can do all things;
no plan of yours can be thwarted."
JOB 42:1–2

God of All Power, in Your goodness and wisdom, You work all things for our benefit, but sometimes we act as if we know best. Whenever our plans crumble, dear God, remind us that Yours never do. Whenever our goals must be modified, changed, or abandoned, assure us again that You have the strength and power to overcome all obstacles when it comes to bringing us ever closer to You. Amen.

Praising Jesus

Let us fix our eyes on Jesus, the author and perfecter of our faith.
HEBREWS 12:2

*L*ord Jesus, we praise and thank You for the gift of our love, the gift of our marriage, and the gift of our life together. Anything we plan or desire pales in comparison to the love You have for both of us! Keep us close to each other and close to You, the true happiness of our home. Amen.

A Prayer for Self-Control

All those who compete in the games use self-control so they can win a crown. That crown is an earthly thing that lasts only a short time, but our crown will never be destroyed.
1 CORINTHIANS 9:25 NCV

*D*ear Father in heaven, how well You know us and how easily we lose sight of our desire to rest at ease in Your presence! For all the impulses of thought, word, and action that shift our eyes away from You, forgive us. Together in heart and mind, keep us focused on You and the crown that is ours through Jesus. Amen.

Give Us Courage

I eagerly expect and hope that I will in no way be ashamed,
but will have sufficient courage so that now as always Christ
will be exalted in my body, whether by life or by death.
For to me, to live is Christ and to die is gain.
PHILIPPIANS 1:20–21

*O*ur Lord God, all things are under Your control, and Your wisdom far surpasses anything we've experienced in this life. When we face disappointment, frustration, a bad outcome, or an unexpected turn of events, give us courage. Teach us to take heart in the certainty of our highest goal: eternal life in You. Amen.

Our Identities

The Power of Knowing Who You Are

It's in Christ that we find out who we are and what we are living for.
Ephesians 1:11 MSG

*T*here is no threat of identity theft in God's economy. That's because God doesn't identify His children by social security numbers, credit ratings, bank account balances, or age. Romans 9:27–28 says, "If each grain of sand on the seashore were numbered and the sum labeled 'chosen of God,' they'd be numbers still, not names; salvation comes by personal selection. God doesn't count us; he calls us by name. Arithmetic is not his focus" (MSG).

People may believe their identity is made up of things like family name, accomplishments, income bracket, talents, appearance, or occupation. But these are merely descriptors—things that paint a picture of what people are like. Who people really are—their true identities—can only be found in who God created them to be.

Even though two become one in marriage, each spouse remains a unique creation to God—a masterpiece of His own miraculous design. For us to better understand our own God-given identity, we need to look beyond what we can see with our eyes. We need to look to Christ.

Ephesians 1:11 says, "It's in Christ that we find out who we are and what we are living for" (MSG). Discovering the depth and breadth of one's true identity is not something that happens overnight. It is a journey that takes a lifetime. Through reading God's Word, bits and pieces are revealed. Scripture proclaims that each of God's individual children are salt (Matthew 5:13), light (Matthew 5:14), a temple (1 Corinthians 6:19), a priest (1 Peter 2:5), and a treasured possession (Deuteronomy 7:6), who without God's life-giving touch would be nothing more than dust. Psalm 103:14 says, "He knows how we were made; he remembers that we are dust" (NRSV).

By living out what scripture reveals about our general identities in Christ, we as God's children can further uncover the intricacies of our personal identities. As husbands and wives pray their way through challenges, opportunities, victories, failures, and the daily ins and outs of married life, we can come to know ourselves, our heavenly Father, and our spouses in a deeper, more authentic way.

Unfortunately, not everyone discovers the true scope of their identity within their lifetime. You do not need to be counted among their numbers. You can choose to live your lives proactively, reveling in a journey of discovery. That may seem like an overwhelming task, but the steps are fairly simple. Talk to God. Take scripture to heart. Act on what God says is true about you. Dare to live up to who you were created to be—and encourage your spouse to do the same. No other two individuals can fill the unique place in this world, and in history, that God has designed for the two of you.

Thanks for Who We Are

*This is what the LORD says. . . "Fear not, for I have redeemed you;
I have summoned you by name; you are mine."*
ISAIAH 43:1

*D*ear Lord, we come before You today with sincere gratitude for who we are—a man and a woman called, redeemed, embraced, and loved by You ever since the world began. Let this sacred knowledge stand firmly at the center of our identities. In our speech, beliefs, and behavior, let us remember always who we are and whose we are. Amen.

We Are God's Children

*[Paul said,] " 'In him we live and move and have our being'; as even
some of your own poets have said, 'For we too are his offspring.' "*
ACTS 17:28 NRSV

*D*ear Father in heaven, in Your love, You have given us the identity of God's children. This great and holy status is far more than we could imagine or ever deserve, yet You have spoken, and it is true. Our most precious possession is the knowledge and the certainty that we belong to You. Amen.

We Are God's Heirs

When we cry, "Abba! Father!" it is that very Spirit bearing witness with our spirit that we are children of God, and if children, then heirs, heirs of God and joint heirs with Christ—if, in fact, we suffer with him so that we may also be glorified with him.
ROMANS 8:15–17 NRSV

*A*bba Father, You have named us members of Your kingdom, making us heirs of Christ's glory and righteousness. As we contemplate these great riches, help us accept the difficulties we encounter, as Christ accepted the cross on our behalf. Amen.

We Are Ambassadors for Christ

We are ambassadors for Christ, since God is making his appeal through us; we entreat you on behalf of Christ, be reconciled to God.
2 CORINTHIANS 5:20 NRSV

*L*ord Jesus, You have honored us by calling us Your son and Your daughter, and You bless us further by identifying us as Your ambassadors. With the help of Your Holy Spirit, help us live according to this high honor and privilege, constantly ready to share Your gospel message with others. Amen.

We Are a New Creation

*If anyone is in Christ, there is a new creation: everything
old has passed away; see, everything has become new!*
2 CORINTHIANS 5:17 NRSV

*D*ear Lord, You renew our spirits and refresh our souls each time
we come to You in prayer. You cease to recall our old identities,
and instead see us as You have made us—a new creation, holy
and righteous in Your sight. Amen.

We Are the Lord's Possession

*If we live, we live to the Lord, and if we die, we die to the Lord;
so then, whether we live or whether we die, we are the Lord's.*
ROMANS 14:8 NRSV

*L*ord Jesus Christ, our identity as Your possession frees us from
needless anxiety about our lives, our circumstances, our present,
and our future. Whatever happens, we rely on the sure and certain
promise that we belong to You now and for eternity. Amen.

We Are God's Workmanship

We are God's workmanship, created in Christ Jesus to do good works,
which God prepared in advance for us to do.
EPHESIANS 2:10

*D*ear God, as a potter sculpts a cup or an artist creates an image, so You have formed us and identified us as Your workmanship. With this sacred identity in mind, we know each of us has a God-given purpose in life, and both of us are precious to You and Your eternal plans. We give thanks to You, Creator God! Amen.

We Are God's People

O come, let us worship and bow down, let us kneel before the Lord, our Maker! For he is our God, and we are the people of his pasture, and the sheep of his hand.
PSALM 95:6–7 NRSV

Almighty Lord God, what comfort we take in knowing we can identify ourselves as Your people! As Your people, we rest in Your protection and providence, work under Your counsel and purpose, and live in joyful expectation of eternal life. Keep us always, Lord God, as citizens of Your kingdom. Amen.

We Are the Sheep of God's Pasture

Know that the Lord is God. It is he that made us, and we are his; we are his people, and the sheep of his pasture.
PSALM 100:3 NRSV

Shepherd of Our Souls, lead us, guide us, guard us, and preserve us as the sheep of Your pasture, for we are easily led astray and unaware of the dangers around us. Let us never become too proud to identify ourselves as Your sheep, and make us ever thankful that You have called us and brought us into the shelter of Your love. Amen.

We Are Known by God

*"Before I formed you in the womb I knew you,
and before you were born I consecrated you."*
JEREMIAH 1:5 NRSV

*C*reator God and Father, thank You for the gift of Your Word. In it we receive knowledge of our identities as people called by You before we were born. No matter what the events of our lives have brought us or will bring, You have given us each other and a life of meaning and purpose. Amen.

We Are Chosen by God

You are a chosen people, a royal priesthood, a holy nation,
a people belonging to God, that you may declare the praises of
him who called you out of darkness into his wonderful light.
1 Peter 2:9

*L*ord God, with profound humility, we ponder the fact that You have chosen us to belong to You. You have graciously shone the light of Your Word on us, assured us of Your love, and identified us as Your chosen people. Let us respond with gladness and gratitude, looking always for ways to praise You in our marriage and daily lives. Amen.

We Are Called to Live by Faith

I have been crucified with Christ; it is no longer I who live,
but Christ lives in me; and the life which I now live in the flesh I live
by faith in the Son of God, who loved me and gave Himself for me.
Galatians 2:20 nkjv

*C*hrist Jesus, You sent Your Spirit to live in us. Grant us a firm commitment to the gospel message and a sincere desire to live by faith in You. In this faith, let us find our identities and recognize You in each other, today and throughout all our days together. Amen.

We Are Bought with a Price

Do you not know that your body is a temple of the Holy Spirit within you, which you have from God, and that you are not your own? For you were bought with a price; therefore glorify God in your body.
1 CORINTHIANS 6:19–20 NRSV

*L*ord God, You have bought us with the price of Your suffering and death, and now You shower on us the benefit of Your resurrection—a free and joyful relationship with You. In You we dedicate ourselves to a clean, healthy, and wholesome lifestyle that honors the price You paid for us. Amen.

We Are Made in God's Image

God created humankind in his image, in the image of God he created them; male and female he created them.
GENESIS 1:27 NRSV

*C*reator God, we look to You for our identities because You are our Creator, shaping us in Your own image. Though weakened by the effects of sin, we look to You for our strength and inspiration. Put Your Word in our hearts, gracious God, and help us live as the man and the woman You created us to be. Amen.

Our Partnership

The Power of Working Together

In the new life of God's grace, you're equals.
Treat your wives, then, as equals so your prayers don't run aground.
1 PETER 3:7 MSG

Solitaire may be a great card game, but it's no way to live a life. God designed people to live in communities, to aid one another, teach one another, and learn how to love one another. Ecclesiastes 4:9–12 expounds on just a few of the reasons why two are better than one: "Two people are better off than one, for they can help each other succeed. If one person falls, the other can reach out and help. But someone who falls alone is in real trouble. Likewise, two people lying close together can keep each other warm. But how can one be warm alone? A person standing alone can be attacked and defeated, but two can stand back-to-back and conquer" (NLT).

Church is one place where children of God are challenged to live in partnership. In the New Testament, the Greek word for partnership is often interchangeable with the word for fellowship. But the original partnership, the very first community God formed, was marriage. In Genesis 2, right after God created Adam, He declared, "It is not good for the man to be alone." Then God created Eve to be Adam's companion, helper, and partner.

Marriage is a unique partnership that leads husbands and wives to fulfill a number of roles. These can include cheerleader, parent, lover, mechanic, cook, counselor, chauffeur, housekeeper, tech support, financial adviser, and lifelong friend. But what sets marriage apart from all other partnerships is the longevity and exclusivity God has established as an essential part of the relationship. When business partners disagree on a course of action or are having difficulty working together, the partnership can be dissolved. But husbands and wives are partners on a much deeper level—a spiritual level that melds two into one. God encourages marital partners to rely on love, not law, to settle their differences.

Sometimes love can be hard work. It can involve sacrifice. It can mean putting someone else's needs before your own. But love pays great dividends. By the same token, when you fail to treat your spouse lovingly, more is affected than your relationship with each other. Your relationship with God is also at risk. In 1 Peter 3:7 we read, "You husbands must give honor to your wives. Treat your wife with understanding as you live together. She may be weaker than you are, but she is your equal partner in God's gift of new life. Treat her as you should so your prayers will not be hindered" (NLT). Though this verse is directed toward husbands, it is reasonable to assume that if wives do not treat their husbands as they should, their communication with God may be hindered as well. Marriage is actually a three-way partnership between a man, a woman, and God. It's a partnership held together with love and prayer.

Holy Partners

Holy partners in a heavenly calling, consider that Jesus, the apostle and high priest of our confession, was faithful to the one who appointed him, just as Moses also "was faithful in all God's house."
HEBREWS 3:1–2 NRSV

*H*eavenly Father, You have called men and women to come together as holy partners, united and faithful to one another. As our love for each other and for You grows deeper and stronger, grant us the understanding, wisdom, and power to honor our sacred calling in thought, word, and action. Amen.

Partners with Christ

[Jesus said,] "Where two or three come together in my name, there am I with them."
MATTHEW 18:20

*L*ord Jesus, bless our marriage and our home with Your presence. With Your Spirit at work in our hearts, keep both of us in true partnership one with another, and in eternal partnership with You, our Lord and our God. Amen.

Fully United

Bear with each other and forgive whatever grievances you may have against one another. Forgive as the Lord forgave you. And over all these virtues put on love, which binds them all together in perfect unity.
COLOSSIANS 3:13–14

*D*ear Lord, we have promised to love each other, yet time and circumstance often work against the love You desire us to enjoy. Open our hearts, Lord, and teach us how to forgive each other, how to restore and renew our partnership, and how to remain fully united in our love for each other and for You. Amen.

Two Are Better Than One

Two are better than one, because they have a good return for their work.
ECCLESIASTES 4:9

*D*ear God, two are better than one, so You gave husband to wife and wife to husband. Teach us to depend on each other for help, understanding, and encouragement. Let us learn to lean on each other for comfort and care. May we find delight in turning to the other as spouse, partner, and friend. Amen.

Fighting the Good Fight

Pursue righteousness, godliness, faith, love, endurance and gentleness.
Fight the good fight of the faith.
1 TIMOTHY 6:11–12

*L*ord God, when challenges arise in our lives and in our marriage, help us keep our focus on You—not on our feelings and problems. Grant us the will and the power to remain strong in our partnership and fight the good fight for godliness and faithfulness, purity and truth. Let our response to the obstacles we face show our unity and serve as an example to all those around us. Amen.

Living in Agreement

Agree with one another so that there may
be no divisions among you.
1 CORINTHIANS 1:10

*L*ord God, when the two of us hold opposing views, plans, and desires, help us to resolve our differences in partnership with You. Let Your Spirit enter our hearts so our conversation remains respectful and kind. In all our doings, show us how to live in agreement with each other, and most important, in conformity with Your Word and Your will. Amen.

United Effort

Make every effort to keep the unity of the Spirit.
EPHESIANS 4:3

*G*od of Unity, we place ourselves and our partnership under the watchful eye of Your Holy Spirit. Guide us as we work to discern Your will for us, and keep us united in constant and diligent effort to live in obedience to Your Word. Amen.

One in Christ

There is neither Jew nor Greek, slave nor free,
male nor female, for you are all one in Christ Jesus.
GALATIANS 3:28

*G*od of heaven and earth, we come before You to ask that You protect our partnership from a desire to wield power over the other. Keep us mindful of our equal place at the foot of Your throne and under the authority of Your Word. Grant us this, we pray, so we may remain one in Christ, our King. Amen.

Building Our Faith

*[Trials] have come so that your faith — of greater worth than gold,
which perishes even though refined by fire — may be proved genuine and
may result in praise, glory and honor when Jesus Christ is revealed.*
1 PETER 1:6–7

*D*ear God, thank You for the challenges present in our lives.
We know that through these challenges, You build our faith,
teaching us to rely ever more on You and on each other. For this
we give You thanks and praise! Amen.

Peaceful Partners

As far as it depends on you, live at peace with everyone.
ROMANS 12:18

*D*ear God, we thank and praise You for the blessing of peace in our relationship with You. Now, we pray that You make us peacemakers, pledging to listen, to ask forgiveness, and to seek harmony. Make us peaceful partners and bless us with a peaceful home and family. Amen.

A Spirit of Unity

May the God who gives endurance and encouragement give you a spirit of unity among yourselves as you follow Christ Jesus.
ROMANS 15:5

*L*ord Jesus, as we learn to follow You together in marriage, provide us with the determination to pursue harmony and seek Your Spirit of unity. Keep us united in partnership with You, with each other, and with an encouraging and supportive faith community. Amen.

Partners Together with the Saints

There is one body and one Spirit—just as you were called to one hope
when you were called—one Lord, one faith, one baptism; one God and
Father of all, who is over all and through all and in all.
EPHESIANS 4:4–6

*A*lmighty God, we come to You in gratitude for the privilege of partnership. Not only have You united us in marriage but through our faith in Jesus Christ as well. Let us live each day mindful of our exalted place as partners together with the saints in heaven and on earth. Amen.

Faces like Flint

Because the Sovereign LORD helps me, I will not be disgraced. Therefore
have I set my face like flint, and I know I will not be put to shame.
ISAIAH 50:7

*S*overeign Lord, though many fear when troubles arise, we put our trust in You and put our fears aside. No matter how many challenges threaten our marriage, home, or family, You are with us and will keep our partnership strong. Help us always to remember that no matter what, You are in control. Amen.

So the World Will Know

"I pray also for those who will believe in me. . . .
May they also be in us so that the world may
believe that you have sent me."
JOHN 17:20–21

Lord Jesus, in Your great love, You have given us each other in holy partnership for our benefit, pleasure, and well-being. Now teach us how to reach out to others in faith and unity so they will know You have blessed us, and through this realization, come to believe in You as Lord and Savior. Amen.

Our Attitudes

The Power of a Right Heart

Don't be selfish; don't try to impress others. Be humble,
thinking of others as better than yourselves. Don't look out
only for your own interests, but take an interest in others, too.
You must have the same attitude that Christ Jesus had.
PHILIPPIANS 2:3–5 NLT

*T*o have the same attitude as Jesus Christ is a pretty tall order. Jesus knew He was God, yet He laid His eternal divinity aside to become a servant to the weak, the hurting, and the oppressed—even to those who were self-centered, arrogant, or cruel. Then He went a step further: He willingly gave His own life in exchange for the lives of those who loved Him, as well as for those who didn't.

A humble, generous attitude isn't something that can be gained by simply wishing it were so. It's something that grows up from the roots of a proper perspective, from having a God's-eye view of both life and death. Prayer is one way of getting a better grasp on God's perspective. It helps align the heart of one who prays with the heart of the One who is being prayed to.

The Gospels record that although Jesus was divine, He spent a lot of time in prayer talking to God the Father. Jesus even gave His followers an example of how to pray in Matthew 6:9–13: the Lord's Prayer. Verse 12 says, "Forgive us our sins, as we have forgiven those who sin against us" (NLT). Obviously, Jesus did not need to ask to be forgiven, since He never sinned. But for anyone else who's ever prayed, this one line is pivotal when it comes to attitude and perspective.

Forgiveness fosters humility. Recognizing the depth of our own sin is the only way to truly understand the depth of God's grace. Romans 3:23 says that "All have sinned and fall short of the glory of God."

Understanding that both you and your spouse have sinned—and been forgiven—will help a humble, Christlike attitude take root and grow within you. It can help knock down walls of self-righteousness, resentment, criticism, and selfishness, replacing them with patience, grace, kindness, and self-sacrifice. As you pray your way through forgiveness for yourself and others, your perspective will begin to change. In turn, so will your attitude—and your marriage. You'll begin to see yourself and your spouse through kinder, more Christlike eyes. So, take time for an attitude adjustment today. Align your perspective with God's through prayer. Gratefully accept His forgiveness and then pass that forgiveness on to those around you.

A Godly Mental Attitude

Put off your old self, which is being corrupted by its deceitful desires. . .
be made new in the attitude of your minds; and. . .put on the new self,
created to be like God in true righteousness and holiness.
EPHESIANS 4:22–24

Dear Lord, our attitude toward each other and outlook on life is rooted in the contents of our heart and mind. Cleanse us, Lord, from perspectives that work to undermine godly wisdom and emotional health, and grant us the gift of a godly mental attitude firmly rooted in You. Amen.

Renewing the Mind

Be constantly renewed in the spirit of your mind.
EPHESIANS 4:23 AMP

Lord Jesus, through Your life, death, and resurrection, You brought us new life and the help and comfort of Your Holy Spirit. Refresh us daily and renew our minds so we may live, speak, and act with the attitude of a man and a woman redeemed and made holy by You—our Savior and Lord. Amen.

Things Above

Since, then, you have been raised with Christ, set your hearts on things above, where Christ is seated at the right hand of God. Set your minds on things above, not on earthly things.
COLOSSIANS 3:1–2

*A*ll-loving Father, through Your Word, You have revealed to us Your gracious intentions for our lives on earth and given us Your promise of a glorious life in heaven. Teach us to set our hearts on things above, and let our heavenly attitudes work in our favor and the favor of others here below. Amen.

Thanks to God

Let the word of Christ dwell in you richly; teach and admonish one another in all wisdom; and with gratitude in your hearts sing psalms, hymns, and spiritual songs to God. And whatever you do, in word or deed, do everything in the name of the Lord Jesus.
COLOSSIANS 3:16–17 NRSV

*D*ear God, You provide us with so many blessings each day, and we sometimes take them for granted. Through Your Holy Spirit, instill in us hearts of gratitude, so we may come before You, our gracious provider of every good thing, with an attitude of joyful thanksgiving. Amen.

Imitators of God

*Be imitators of God, therefore, as dearly loved children
and live a life of love, just as Christ loved us and gave himself
up for us as a fragrant offering and sacrifice to God.*
EPHESIANS 5:1–2

*D*ear God, just as parents set an example for their children to imitate, so You lovingly invite us to imitate You in our lives. Guide us and empower us as we commit ourselves to living a life of love, beginning with the attitude of our hearts. Change us, all-powerful God, into imitators of You. Amen.

Living as Jesus Did

*Those who obey God's word truly show how completely
they love him. That is how we know we are living him. Those
who say they live in God should live their lives as Jesus did.*
1 JOHN 2:5–7 NLT

*L*oving Lord, You lived a blameless life on earth, setting an amazing example for us to follow. Grant us, we pray, the gift of Your Spirit and a sincere desire to live as You did: obedient in thought, word, action, and attitude. Amen.

Arm Yourselves

*Since therefore Christ suffered in the flesh, arm yourselves also
with the same intention (for whoever has suffered in the flesh has
finished with sin), so as to live for the rest of your earthly life
no longer by human desires but by the will of God.*
1 PETER 4:1–2 NRSV

*C*hrist Jesus, You suffered and died to bring us new life and
show us how to live. With an attitude of thanksgiving for Your
great sacrifice on our behalf, help us arm ourselves against sinful
desires so we may live ever more fully according to Your will.
Amen.

An Attitude of Humility

*By the grace given to me I say to everyone among you not to think of
yourself more highly than you ought to think, but to think with sober
judgment, each according to the measure of faith that God has assigned.*
ROMANS 12:3 NRSV

*D*ear Lord, we're reluctant to put others before ourselves, yet
this is what You require us to do in our marriage and other close
relationships. Grant us, Lord, an attitude of humility toward
others—for any power and authority we possess comes from
You, who intended it to be used for the well-being of others.
Amen.

Becoming like Children

[Jesus said,] "I tell you the truth,
unless you change and become like little children,
you will never enter the kingdom of heaven."
MATTHEW 18:3

*H*eavenly Father, You have graciously opened the kingdom of heaven to us, inviting us in as a loving and compassionate Father. Though our childhood years have passed, renew us with a childlike attitude of wonder, discovery, and awe, and let us adopt an unconditional love for You. Amen.

Giving Up the World

Don't copy the behavior and customs of this world, but let God transform you into a new person by changing the way you think.
ROMANS 12:2 NLT

*G*od of All Grace, we come before You in thanksgiving for the new life You have given us through Jesus Christ. Enable us to gladly turn away from the world's temptations and fully embrace the godly attitude and outlook You would have us possess. Amen.

Putting on the New Self

You have taken off your old self with its practices and have put on the new self, which is being renewed in knowledge in the image of its Creator.
COLOSSIANS 3:9–10

*L*ord Jesus, You have made life in You possible for us, and for this indescribable gift we give You thanks and praise. Bless us, we pray, with a renewed attitude of mind and spirit, clothed in faith and trust in You. Grant each of us the will and the power to put on the new self, a self renewed and restored by You. Amen.

Think about These Things

Whatever is true, whatever is honorable,
whatever is just, whatever is pure, whatever is pleasing,
whatever is commendable, if there is any excellence and if
there is anything worthy of praise, think about these things.
PHILIPPIANS 4:8 NRSV

All-seeing God, You know everything about us, even our most private thoughts. Fill our hearts, therefore, with knowledge and desires that are worthy of our attention. Help us nurture godly attitudes by thinking on all things pure, praiseworthy, true, and pleasing in Your sight. Amen.

What God Requires

What does the LORD require of you?
To act justly and to love mercy and to walk humbly with your God.
MICAH 6:8

*L*ord God, often we are so busy with what we require and what others require that we forget to ask what You require. Instill in us right priorities so we can put Your requirements first. Let our daily attitude show our concern for Your will and our commitment to justice, mercy, and humility in all things. Amen.

Pursuing God's Virtues

As for you, man of God. . .pursue righteousness, godliness,
faith, love, endurance, gentleness. . . . Take hold of the eternal life,
to which you were called and for which you made the good
confession in the presence of many witnesses.
1 TIMOTHY 6:11–12 NRSV

*G*racious God, You have given us the power to pursue godly virtues for the purpose of reflecting our faith and helping others. Draw us closer and closer to You in our attitude, choices, words, and actions, and grant us the privilege of sharing the glory of Your love in our lives. Amen.

Our Finances

The Power of the Bottom Line

*Keep your lives free from the love of money and be content
with what you have, because God has said,
"Never will I leave you; never will I forsake you."*
HEBREWS 13:5

*N*o one falls madly in love with a socket wrench. After all,
it's just a tool. It's handy to have around if something needs
to be tightened or loosened, but that's about it. Once the job
is finished, the wrench goes back in the toolbox. It isn't kept
close at hand to help cook dinner, change a diaper, or give a
massage. It can only do what it was designed to do—handle
nuts and bolts.

In the same way, money is just a tool. It can only be used
in exchange for goods and services. It can be used to purchase
a socket wrench, but it's useless when it comes to loosening a
rusted bolt or cooking dinner on its own. That's not its job.

The value of money is derived from what the treasury
and economy say it's worth. But many of us link our worth
to what's found in our wallets. Our security, happiness, and
sometimes even our identities lie in how much we are "worth"
on paper. When this happens, money is no longer a tool. It has
become a god.

Jesus spoke very directly on this subject. He said, "No one
can serve two masters. Either he will hate the one and love the

other, or he will be devoted to the one and despise the other. You cannot serve both God and Money" (Matthew 6:24).

Money can become a master in quietly cunning ways. So cunning, that placing our trust in money instead of God can appear to be financially responsible—at least from the outside. But it's what going on in our hearts that makes all the difference. Discontentment is one telltale sign that money has become a master. Ecclesiastes 5:10 says, "Whoever loves money never has money enough; whoever loves wealth is never satisfied with his income."

Has a love of money crept into your marriage? If discontent over your monthly income, where you live, the kind of car you drive, or the size of your retirement fund are common conversations between you and your spouse, it may be time to take a good look at where your loyalties really lie. Stress and anxiety over money can be warning signs pointing to a deeper problem.

Make it a habit to pray before you pay. . .ask God for His guidance and wisdom in how to save, spend, and give away what He has so generously given you. Keep in mind that your finances are really God's resources and that He has entrusted you to invest them wisely.

Avoiding Financial Grief

*For the love of money is a root of all kinds of evil.
Some people, eager for money, have wandered from
the faith and pierced themselves with many griefs.*
1 TIMOTHY 6:10

*D*ear Father, help us as we try to ease the grip money has on our lives. Instead of riches, we ask for contentment. Keep our hearts in check and our lives properly balanced between earning what we need and striving to satisfy our wants. We ask for Your guidance day by day to keep us tuned in to You and turned off to greed. Amen.

The Measure of a Life

*[Jesus] said to them, "Watch out! Be on your guard against all kinds of
greed; a man's life does not consist in the abundance of his possessions."*
LUKE 12:15

*H*eavenly Father, it's easy in our culture to think that you are no one if you don't have the latest gadgets or fashions. We know better, and yet we often feel our hearts pulled in that direction. Remind us daily that possessions can be gone in a moment, but Your love will always be with us. Amen.

God Gives Wealth

Remember the LORD your God, for it is he who gives you the
ability to produce wealth, and so confirms his covenant,
which he swore to your forefathers, as it is today.
DEUTERONOMY 8:18

*D*ear Lord, everything we have has come from You. Though we work hard, we know that You have given us the skills and talents necessary to carry out our jobs and provided us with the opportunities to use them to develop the income that takes care of our needs. We are ever grateful for Your gracious help. Amen.

Putting God First

"Seek the kingdom of God,
and all these things shall be added to you."
LUKE 12:31 NKJV

*H*eavenly Father, thank You for reminding us that Your ability to meet our needs has much to do with our ability to hear Your voice and act wisely in the affairs of this life. No wonder You tell us to put our relationship with You first to ensure that we are always in a position to receive Your blessings and Your help. You are indeed a gracious God. Amen.

God Will Supply

*My God will meet all your needs according
to his glorious riches in Christ Jesus.*
PHILIPPIANS 4:19

Lord of Abundance, You have promised to take care of us in good times and in bad times. That promise means so much to us. We know that even those who have accumulated great riches could lose it all in one day. Nothing is secure—except You. You know the beginning and the end, and Your resources are unlimited. We put our faith in You as we go about the business of providing for those we love. Amen.

All We Need

*God is able to make all grace abound to you, so that in all things at all
times, having all that you need, you will abound in every good work.*
2 CORINTHIANS 9:8

Wonderful Father, You are exactly what a good father should be: someone who loves and cares for his family, and we are grateful for Your loving care and provision. We know You bless our finances. You show us ways to stretch and multiply what we have during the hard times and ways to better enjoy what we have during the good times. Thank You, Lord. Amen.

Pursuing Contentment

I know what it is to be in need, and I know what it is to have plenty.
I have learned the secret of being content in any and every situation,
whether well fed or hungry, whether living in plenty or in want.
PHILIPPIANS 4:12

*L*ord God, thank You for helping us sort out our needs from our wants. We know You don't begrudge us the joy of having something nice now and then, but we ask Your forgiveness for those times when we failed to consult You because we knew You would disapprove. Thank You for helping us spend more wisely. Amen.

Being Satisfied

Whoever loves wealth is never satisfied with his income.
ECCLESIASTES 5:10

*F*ather God, we wish to be satisfied with the blessings You have given us. We ask You to monitor our hearts, warning us when we become fixated on what others have. We want to love You rather than money, and we want to live our lives knowing that the most wonderful things in life can't be bought for a price. Amen.

Giving Back to God

*Honor the Lord with your wealth, with the firstfruits
of all your crops; then your barns will be filled to overflowing,
and your vats will brim over with new wine.*
PROVERBS 3:9–10

*H*oly Father, we want to honor You with our finances—not because we have to or because we expect extra blessings in return, but because we want to give back to You as freely and generously as You have given to us. Thank You for all You have placed in our hands. Amen.

Resolute Giving

Each man should give what he has decided in his heart to give, not reluctantly or under compulsion, for God loves a cheerful giver.
2 CORINTHIANS 9:7

*H*eavenly Father, when it comes to finances, we want to have hearts worthy of passing Your blessings on to others. We ask You to nudge us when there is a need to fill, and we thank You for the opportunity to be Your cheerful, enthusiastic, and obedient servants. Amen.

The Reward of Giving

"Give, and it will be given to you. A good measure, pressed down, shaken together and running over, will be poured into your lap. For with the measure you use, it will be measured to you."
LUKE 6:38

*L*ord God, as always with You, there are blessings piled upon blessings. When we give back out of devotion and gratitude, You pile even more blessings on us. How awesome You are! Everything we know about being generous, faithful, and sensitive to the needs of others, we have learned from You. Thank You, Lord. Amen.

Financial Responsibility

*Make it your ambition to lead a quiet life, to mind your own
business and to work with your hands, just as we told you,
so that your daily life may win the respect of outsiders
and so that you will not be dependent on anybody.*
1 THESSALONIANS 4:11–12

*L*ord God, we know that money is just money, but it is an
important necessity here on earth. We need it to care for ourselves
and our family and to carry out Your will here on earth. Thank
You for making us responsible stewards of this worldly tool.
Amen.

Watching God Bless

He who gathers money little by little makes it grow.
PROVERBS 13:11

*F*ather God, we want to be responsible stewards not only in
our giving but also in our own financial decisions. Give us the
wisdom to save for the future and the patience to set aside our
wants for those things that You say are important. More than
anything else, we want the way we manage our finances to be
pleasing to You. Amen.

A Life of Faithfulness

*"Whoever can be trusted with a little
can also be trusted with a lot."*
LUKE 16:10 NCV

Father God, show us how to be vessels of blessing to others. Teach us how to be Your earthly hands, providing for those who are in need of help and hope. Make us sensitive to Your voice, and we promise to be faithful and trustworthy channels of finance for You. Amen.

Our Time

The Power of a Day Well Spent

*There's an opportune time to do things,
a right time for everything on the earth.*
ECCLESIASTES 3:1 MSG

*T*he question, "What would Jesus do?" has become a catch-phrase synonymous with making a wise decision. But in pondering that question, we are ultimately asking ourselves, "How would Jesus choose to spend His time?" While here on earth, Jesus was under the same time constraints as the rest of mankind. He had twenty-four hours in each day throughout a life that was bordered by birth and death—just like we do.

Though scripture doesn't provide an hour-by-hour replay of Jesus' daily schedule, the end of the second chapter of the Gospel of Luke lets readers know that Jesus led a balanced life. In other words, it shows that Jesus used his time well. Luke 2:52 says, "Jesus grew in wisdom and stature, and in favor with God and men." The time of growth this verse occurs between the time Jesus was found in the temple by His parents at age twelve and when He began His public ministry, around the age of thirty. To grow in "wisdom and stature," Jesus needed to spend time caring for His mind and His body. To grow "in favor with God and men," Jesus needed to spend time nurturing relationships with His Father in heaven and with people here on earth. And if Jesus was growing in "favor with God," undoubtedly God approved of how Jesus was spending the time He'd been given.

Obviously there is much more that needs accomplished in a day besides taking time to care for one's mind, body, and relationships. Meals need to be made. Laundry needs to be washed. Bills need to be paid. Tasks need to be accomplished at work. All the odds and ends of making a living take up a large portion of each and every day. That's where Luke 2:52 can serve as a touchstone on how to spend time wisely. It's a reminder that it takes more than "making a living" to make a life.

How you spend your time will ultimately determine how you spend your life. If you want to spend your time well, you first need to be aware of what you are spending your time on. Then, with thought, prayer, and a plan of action, you and your spouse can choose what to say "yes" and "no" to when scheduling your day. Scheduling some time to nurture your heart (your relationships with others), your soul (your relationship with God), your mind (both wisdom and knowledge), and your strength (your physical body) each and every day will help you lead a more balanced life—a life that will continually grow in favor with God and others.

Eternity in Our Hearts

[God] has made everything beautiful in its time.
He has also set eternity in the hearts of men; yet they
cannot fathom what God has done from beginning to end.
ECCLESIASTES 3:11

*D*ear Father, You have set eternity in our hearts. How wonderful that is! We human beings are so tied to time, but now we are able to think as You think: broadly, open-endedly. We are able to see past the limitations of this life and imagine all of our tomorrows with You. Amen.

A Proper Time

There is a proper time and procedure for every matter.
ECCLESIASTES 8:6

*H*oly Lord, You have brought planning and structure to our lives where there was once only chaos. We were drifting, but You have pointed us in the right direction and given us a reason to live. Thank You for giving our lives purpose and helping us align our desires with Yours to accomplish Your will. Amen.

Time and Chance

*The race is not to the swift or the battle to the strong,
nor does food come to the wise or wealth to the brilliant or
favor to the learned; but time and chance happen to them all.*
ECCLESIASTES 9:11

*F*ather God, we understand that by living in this world, we are subject to its forces. If the ground shakes, we shake, too. When the rain falls, we get wet. But we also know a secret: Though we are subject to time and chance, You turn every circumstance for our good. You are a great God. Amen.

Making Prayer a Priority

My intercessor is my friend as my eyes pour out tears to God.
JOB 16:20

*F*ather, remind us to make it a priority to pray for the people and the needs we see around us. Bring these things to our attention on a daily basis. Teach us to be intercessors for those we love. And, Lord, we are thankful that You have given so many of our friends the desire to pray for us. We feel their prayers each day, strengthening and comforting us. Amen.

Ministry to the Least

"The King will reply, 'I tell you the truth, whatever you did
for one of the least of these brothers of mine, you did for me.'"
MATTHEW 25:40

*L*ord Jesus, You told Your disciples that You came to serve, and You set an example by paying attention to the pleas, feelings, and needs of those who were considered insignificant and unimportant. With You as our example, let us never turn away from humble service. Help us embrace it with joy, for whatever we do for those in need, we do for You. Amen.

Every Minute

These are evil times, so make every minute count.
EPHESIANS 5:16 CEV

*S*weet Lord, our length of time here on earth is not known to us. But we are comforted to recall that You do know. You've counted every minute—even before our birth. When the world around us is shaking, we will trust in Your goodness and faithfulness. We give every one of our days, hours, and minutes to You. Amen.

The Time Is Now

*God says, "At the right time I heard your prayers.
On the day of salvation I helped you." I tell you that the
"right time" is now, and the "day of salvation" is now.*
2 CORINTHIANS 6:2 NCV

*L*ord and Savior, thank You for hearing us when we called to You. We were drowning in our sins, but You quickly lifted us up and put our feet on solid ground. You didn't hesitate—not for a moment. Our only regret is that we waited so long to reach out to You and declare that beautiful "day of salvation." Amen.

Wellness for the Soul

Beloved, I pray that all may go well with you and that you may be in good health, just as it is well with your soul.
3 JOHN 1:2 NRSV

*F*ather, we know it is Your will for us to be well in every way physically, mentally, emotionally, and spiritually. Show us ways we can use our time to improve our well-being, whether that includes walking more or reading the Bible more or dealing with issues in our lives more effectively. We love You, Lord. Amen.

The Right Time

You see, at just the right time, when we were still powerless, Christ died for the ungodly.
ROMANS 5:6

*L*ord God, though we waited, foolishly delaying, You did not wait. You sent Your Son, Jesus, to sacrifice His life for ours even before we knew we needed a Savior. You acted at just the right time in just the right way to bring us to just the right place of repentance and rebirth. Amen.

Being Wise

The wise mind will know the time and way.
ECCLESIASTES 8:5 NRSV

*H*eavenly Father, we need Your help as we endeavor to be wise with our time. We want to use each hour and each minute for the purpose You intended. Give us the discernment to see when we are involving ourselves in something that will squander our time and make us unproductive. We want everything we do to count for Your kingdom. Amen.

An Opportune Time

There's an opportune time to do things,
a right time for everything on the earth.
ECCLESIASTES 3:1 MSG

*F*ather God, as we quiet our hearts and set our schedule before You, we look to You for each and every decision—when to change jobs, when to invest our money, when to confront certain situations, when to be tender, and when to be tough. We know we won't always do this perfectly, but our hearts are determined to follow You as closely as we can, and with Your help we hope to make a difference. Amen.

Time to Find God

"The Lord is with you, while you are with him.
If you seek him, he will be found by you."
2 CHRONICLES 15:2 NRSV

*L*ord God, we pray for those who have not yet found the joy of having You in their lives. We ask You to draw them to You, open their hearts, and awaken a desire in them for something more than this world can offer. Give us words to answer their questions and inspire hope in them—the hope that if they seek You, You will be waiting to pour out Your love on them. Amen.

Time to Draw Near to God

Draw near to God, and he will draw near to you.
JAMES 4:8 NRSV

*F*ather God, as we pray for others, we pray also for ourselves. We know that as human beings we are prone to wander. We are counting on You to watch over us as a shepherd watches over his sheep. Keep us in the fold. We are grateful for Your promise that You will always be there when we look for You. Amen.

Finding Mercy

Seek the Lord while he may be found. . .let the wicked forsake their way, and the unrighteous their thoughts; let them return to the Lord, that he may have mercy on them.
ISAIAH 55:6–7 NRSV

*H*eavenly Father, we thank You for pouring out Your mercy on our marriage. We know how often we fail to measure up to the standards You've set for us, but You are always ready to set us back on the right path. Guard our hearts and minds against unrighteous thoughts, replacing them with memories of all You have done for us. Amen.

Our Church

The Power of Risking Relationship

You are the body of Christ, and each one of you is a part of it.
1 CORINTHIANS 12:27

A marriage can be like a mini-church. A husband and wife pray for one another, encourage one another, read scripture together, and may even come together in song to praise God. In Matthew 18:20, Jesus said, "Where two or three come together in my name, there am I with them." However, every couple also needs to be involved in a larger family of God. Becoming part of a local church congregation provides spiritual oversight by a pastor, fellowship with those who share your faith, instruction from the Word of God, the inspiration of corporate worship, and much more. It should be a warm and comfortable place where your individuality and your coupleness can find expression as part of something greater than yourselves.

Every local church body is unique. First Corinthians 12:12–31 describes the church in "body" terminology, where some members are compared to hands, others to feet or eyes or ears. In the human body, if a part is missing, the whole body is affected. The part cannot function on its own without the body, and without that missing part, the body cannot function the way God designed it to. On the contrary, when all the parts work together, things can be accomplished that no single part, or incomplete body, could accomplish on its own.

As a group, members of a church can support one another with their wide variety of unique gifts. They can pray, encourage, aid, challenge, and teach each other. They also have more hands (literally) with which they can extend God's love to their community and the world. And when it comes to learning what it means to really love, members of a church body are put into a perfect position where they have to learn to work together.

It could be you have already found just the right church, but if not, be encouraged. God does have a place where you can make your unique contribution. Agree together in prayer that He will show you just where He wants you to be. After all, He led you to each other and He will faithfully lead you to a church family as well.

Once you know you are where God wants you to be, join in with all your hearts. Take every opportunity to listen as the Word of God is taught. Enter in with your songs and praises as the congregation worships together. Spend time with your sisters and brothers in the Lord. In the process, you will find your relationship with God gaining strength and momentum and your marriage reaching new levels of meaning and purpose.

Christ Is the Head

[Christ] is the head of the body, the church;
he is the beginning and the firstborn from among the dead,
so that in everything he might have the supremacy.
COLOSSIANS 1:18

*L*ord of heaven and earth, we exalt You in all things and praise You for Your Son, Jesus, who is the head of Your church. We promise to seek Him and obey Your commandments, devoting ourselves to the purposes set before us. We place Him first in our hearts, first in our marriage, and first in our lives. Amen.

The Christ-Filled Church

The church is filled with Christ,
and Christ fills everything in every way.
EPHESIANS 1:23 NCV

*F*ather God, how wonderful it is to be part of what You are doing here on earth. You have bound us together and given us the power to carry out Your work. You have united us in heart and mind and filled each of us with the purity and passion of Your precious Son, Jesus. May our marriage and our lives be a reflection of the goals You desire to achieve on earth. Amen.

Christ's Body

The body is a unit, though it is made up of many parts. . . .
So it is with Christ. For we were all baptized by one Spirit into
one body—whether Jews or Greeks, slave or free—
and we were all given the one Spirit to drink.
1 CORINTHIANS 12:12–13

*D*ear Father, here we are all thinking and acting differently, but Your commandment for us is to be as one. Give us the grace to look past petty differences and believe that You will align our hearts with the work You have called us to do. Amen.

Many Members

Just as each of us has one body with many members, and these members
do not all have the same function, so in Christ we who are many form
one body, and each member belongs to all the others.
ROMANS 12:4–5

*S*weet Lord, we look around us and rejoice at the diversity You created. You never wanted a body of believers who all looked alike, thought alike, and acted alike. You revel in our differences, and becoming one in vision and purpose does not mean that You want us to become the same. Thank You for guarding our uniqueness. Amen.

God's Household

You are. . .members of God's household, built on the foundation of the apostles and prophets, with Christ Jesus himself as the chief cornerstone. In him the whole building is joined together and rises to become a holy temple in the Lord.
EPHESIANS 2:19–21

Lord God, how wonderful it is that You have brought so many different people from every corner of the earth to be citizens in Your kingdom. We are all equals here, brought together to carry out Your purposes on earth. We are so privileged to be part of Your holy temple. Amen.

A Chosen People

You are a chosen people, a royal priesthood, a holy nation, a people belonging to God, that you may declare the praises of him who called you out of darkness into his wonderful light.
1 PETER 2:9

Heavenly Father, You have called us a chosen people and a royal priesthood. We are a nation whose borders are Your love and grace, Your kindness and forgiveness. Thank You for taking us as we are and making us part of something so wonderful and exciting. Thank You for giving us purpose and hope. Amen.

The Family of God

Even if I am delayed, you will know how to live in the family of God.
That family is the church of the living God,
the support and foundation of the truth.
1 TIMOTHY 3:15 NCV

*F*ather, sometimes it's difficult to translate that greater vision of Your universal church into the doors of a local church, where we must relate to one another on a personal level. Just as we encounter conflict in our marriage, we also encounter conflict in our church family. Teach us how to live in harmony with those You have placed in our lives. Amen.

Strengthen the Church

You are so eager to have the special abilities the Spirit gives,
seek those that will strengthen the whole church.
1 CORINTHIANS 14:12 NLT

*L*ord, we wish to be faithful to Your universal body of believers and to the local fellowship You have called us to on a regular basis. We ask that You would help us use our gifts to strengthen and bless our church body. Please show us ways to help others identify and use their spiritual gifts so that we all might be better equipped to do Your work. Amen.

One Body

And is not the bread that we break a participation in the body of Christ?
Because there is one loaf, we, who are many, are one body,
for we all partake of the one loaf.
1 CORINTHIANS 10:16–17

*L*ord, we are honored to be part of Your body. When we take communion, we remember how You gave Your body and blood for us and that Your sacrifice brought all believers together. We were all without hope in ourselves and in need of saving. We have all come in at a common door—the door of faith and forgiveness. Amen.

One in Christ

There is neither Jew nor Greek, slave nor free,
male nor female, for you are all one in Christ Jesus.
GALATIANS 3:28

*H*eavenly Father, although we are married and You see us as one, we are pleased to know that You also see us as individuals, too, and regardless of our roles, gifts, abilities, and personalities, You love us equally. You see us both as Your children, and You love us just as we are. Thank You, Lord. Amen.

Assemble Together

Let us consider one another in order to stir up love and good works,
not forsaking the assembling of ourselves together,
as is the manner of some, but exhorting one another,
and so much the more as you see the Day approaching.
HEBREWS 10:24–25 NKJV

*L*ord God, remind us each day how important it is to spend time with other members of Your body. We should be praying together as a couple, and we should be inviting others to pray with us as well. Help us remember that we need each other to be complete. Amen.

Teach and Admonish

Let the word of Christ dwell in you richly as you teach and admonish one another with all wisdom, and as you sing psalms, hymns and spiritual songs with gratitude in your hearts to God.
COLOSSIANS 3:16

*F*ather, we know that You have asked us to exercise our gifts and callings together with others, but we are sometimes shy about stepping out. We pray for the courage to take up our role in Your church, whether it be singer, teacher, mentor, or leader. Help us remind others to open their hearts and wholly devote themselves to You. Amen.

The Lord's Blessing

How good and pleasant it is when brothers live together in unity! It is like precious oil poured on the head, running down on the beard. . . . For there the LORD bestows his blessing, even life forevermore.
PSALM 133

*D*ear Lord, we desire Your blessing over our marriage, our home, our nation, and our church body. Teach us how to live in harmony and give us hearts of compassion for one another. Remind us that we are bound together by the will of God and the power of the Holy Spirit. Thank You, Lord, for Your blessing. Amen.

Many Parts

The human body has many parts, but the many parts
make up one whole body. So it is with the body of Christ.
1 CORINTHIANS 12:12 NLT

*F*ather, we are in awe of You. It's amazing to think that You have endowed us all with the necessary gifts to accomplish Your will. Remind us often that everyone in Your body of believers is unique, ourselves included. And when we get frustrated because someone else sees things differently than we do, remind us that their perspective was Your intention all along. Amen.

Our Friendships

The Power of Fellowship

Perfume and incense bring joy to the heart, and the pleasantness
of one's friend springs from his earnest counsel.
PROVERBS 27:9 NIV

*T*he Bible makes it clear that friendship is one of God's most lavish blessings. In fact, it is a blessing inherent in the marriage relationship. The two of you can and should each be the other's best friend, laughing together, confiding in each other, leaning on each other during the difficult times, and enjoying all the goodness of life together.

But God also intended for couples to have friendships outside the bonds of marriage. A well-balanced couple will have close bonds with other couples, and both the husband and wife will have friends of their own.

Since Jesus spent much of His time with friends and turned to them for support during His deepest times of need, we should recognize our own need for a circle of friends. Being married, even to a best friend, does not fill the need for other friendships. Each spouse needs friends of their own to go to for counsel, support, and a good laugh now and then. Proverbs 27:9 says, "The heartfelt counsel of a friend is as sweet as perfume and incense" (NLT).

Counsel that is sweet perfume is counsel that carries the scent of Christ. This does not mean that Christians should only have Christian friends. However, it does mean that when seeking advice, the best place to find it is from a friend whose ear is attentive to God's still, quiet voice.

The more you reach out in love to others, the more likely it is that others will reach out in love to you. Even then, everyone goes through seasons of loneliness in life. If you or your spouse come to a time when a good friend is hard to find, pray for one another. Pray that God will bring the gift of a newfound acquaintance your way. Then keep your eyes and heart open. Be the first to make a move. Invite an acquaintance over for a cup of coffee or on a walk around the block. Begin praying for that person on a regular basis. Allow God to bond your hearts together in His time and way. You never know when you'll meet a lifelong friend for the very first time.

Constant Friends

*A friend is always loyal, and a brother
is born to help in time of need.*
PROVERBS 17:17 NLT

*H*eavenly Father, thank You for the friends we have in our lives. They always seem to be there when we need them to provide encouragement, support, and laughter. Help us to be true and faithful friends in return. We pray that each one of them would be aware of Your presence and a recipient of Your blessings. Amen.

True Friends

*Some friends play at friendship but a true
friend sticks closer than one's nearest kin.*
PROVERBS 18:24 NRSV

*L*ord God, thank You for friends who care about us deeply and who are concerned about our spiritual needs as well as our earthly needs. These friends are Your gifts to us. You use them to show us our blind spots and inspire us to be all You have created us to be. Show us how we can be true friends to them as well. Amen.

Harmonious Friends

*I appeal to you, brothers and sisters, by the name of our Lord Jesus
Christ, that all of you be in agreement and that there be no divisions
among you, but that you be united in the same mind
and the same purpose.*
1 CORINTHIANS 1:10 NRSV

*F*ather, we pray for harmony in our marriage and in our friendships. Help us remember that harmony does not mean thinking and acting exactly the same—it means working together happily and productively and finding characteristics in others that complement our differences. Thank You, Lord, for friends. Amen.

Honoring Friends

*Be devoted to one another in brotherly love.
Honor one another above yourselves.*
ROMANS 12:10

*L*ord, give us hearts of compassion for those around us, loving and honoring them through thick and thin, overlooking offenses, shoring up weak areas, and rejoicing in their strengths. Let us follow the example of Jesus, who is the best friend of all—a friend who never wavers and never fails us. Amen.

Beneficial Friends

As iron sharpens iron, so a friend sharpens a friend.
PROVERBS 27:17 NLT

Lord God, help us remember and appreciate that friendship has two sides. One side encourages and supports us, sees the best in us, and loves us unconditionally. The other side tells us the truth about ourselves, wears down our rough edges, and urges us back onto the right path when we go astray. Thank You for friends who love us enough to push us in the right direction. Amen.

Trusted Friends

Wounds from a friend can be trusted.
PROVERBS 27:6

*G*od our Father, we trust You even when Your words are words of correction. They hurt, but we have confidence that Your advice will help us make the necessary adjustments to our attitudes and behaviors, so we can grow closer to the person we were meant to be. You've given us friends to help deliver Your messages to us. Thank You, Lord, for friends who speak the truth in love. Amen.

Righteous Friends

The righteous should choose his friends carefully,
for the way of the wicked leads them astray.
PROVERBS 12:26 NKJV

*D*ear Father, we know You have brought some wonderful friends into our lives. We find we are often attracted though to people who will not bring us closer to You. Help us to choose friends who are pleasing to You, friends who are living righteous lives— friends who have opened their hearts to You. Amen.

Devoted Friends

A despairing man should have the devotion of his friends,
even though he forsakes the fear of the Almighty.
JOB 6:14

*F*ather God, thank You for friends who are devoted to us, friends who put our needs above their convenience and comfort. They are there when the dog is missing, knocking on doors and searching the neighborhood with us. They are there at the hospital with us, sitting in uncomfortable lounge seats, drinking bad coffee, and eating the cafeteria food. They are always there, loving us no matter what. Thank You, Lord, for friends. Amen.

God's Friends

[Jesus said,] "I have called you friends."
JOHN 15:15 NKJV

*F*ather God, You have called us Your friends. We can barely comprehend that. What a privilege and honor. Thank You for having confidence in us, for wanting us to be part of Your kingdom. Show us how to walk in a way that is pleasing to You—our best friend of all. Amen.

Intimate Friends

*"Greater love has no one than this, that he lay down
his life for his friends. . . . I no longer call you
servants. . .for everything that I learned from
my Father I have made known to you."*
JOHN 15:13–15

*L*ord, thank You for giving us friends whom we can trust with
the private affairs of our lives. They cheer for us in our victories
and cry with us over our disappointments. You have called us
Your friends, Lord. Thank You for allowing us to be part of
Your purposes. Amen.

God-Chosen Friends

These God-chosen lives all around —
what splendid friends they make!
PSALM 16:3 MSG

*H*eavenly Father, those friends You have chosen for us are the best friends of all. They are the ones whom we might never have met, but You caused our paths to cross. These friends set an example of righteous living and are always there when we need them. Thank You, Lord, for these wonderful people we call our friends. Amen.

Fostering Friends

One who forgives an affront fosters friendship,
but one who dwells on disputes will alienate a friend.
PROVERBS 17:9 NRSV

*L*ord God, just as partners in marriage, friends live in close communion with one another. Sometimes we accidentally offend one another, and other times, we are the ones who are offended. We pray You would give us the grace to forgive for the sake of friendship, just as we are forgiven our offenses by others for the same reason. Amen.

Proven Friends

Do not forsake your friend and the friend of your father.
PROVERBS 27:10

*F*ather, it's always fun to find a new friend, and we know it's Your will for us to constantly be adding to our circle of friends. But sometimes we begin to take our longtime friends for granted. We don't appreciate them as much as we do those we are still getting to know. Help us to respect and honor all our friendships. Amen.

Dwelling Together as Friends

Behold, how good and how pleasant it is
for brethren to dwell together in unity!
PSALM 133:1 NKJV

*L*ord God, Your heart must rejoice when You see Your children getting along, working together toward common goals, and honoring and respecting one another. We want to please You, make You proud, and bring joy to Your heart. Thank You for the friends You've brought into our lives. We promise to treat them as Your precious gifts to us, and do all that is in our power to live in harmony with them. Amen.

Our Health

The Power of Well-Being

LORD, heal me, and I will truly be healed.
Save me, and I will truly be saved. You are the one I praise.
JEREMIAH 17:14 NCV

*T*raditional marriage vows ask would-be husbands and wives to commit themselves to one another through several potential seasons of married life: for better or for worse, for richer or for poorer, in sickness and in health. Every couple hopes that the better, richer, healthier seasons of life will outweigh the rest, but when couples remain married until "death do us part," they are bound to go through seasons of ill health along the way. Some may even find themselves facing long-term health issues that make illness a part of daily life.

God cares about the health of His children. Though the Gospels do not record every minute of Jesus' life, the majority of the miracles described in the Gospels show Jesus healing people—the lame, the blind, the mentally unstable, those with leprosy, even those who had already moved beyond sickness into the realm of death. Jesus cared for people's bodies as well as their souls.

Today, miraculous healings are not as commonplace as they were in Jesus' day. But that doesn't mean prayers asking the Great Physician for His healing touch are wasted words. Over and over again, scripture proclaims that God cares about every detail of His children's lives—and He invites His children to pray about each and every one of these details. In answer to these prayers, God may provide healing in unexpected ways.

When the apostle Paul prayed to be healed from what he referred to as "a thorn in my flesh," Paul underwent a miraculous healing of his point of view. In 2 Corinthians 12:8–10, Paul writes regarding his thorn, "Three times I pleaded with the Lord to take it away from me. But he said to me, 'My grace is sufficient for you, for my power is made perfect in weakness.' Therefore I will boast all the more gladly about my weaknesses, so that Christ's power may rest on me. That is why, for Christ's sake, I delight in weaknesses, in insults, in hardships, in persecutions, in difficulties. For when I am weak, then I am strong."

Through the power of prayer, God can take a winterlike season of physical difficulty and transform it into a springtime of new growth and inexplicable joy. No matter what type of healing you or your spouse are in need of, join together in turning to the Lord in prayer—regularly, honestly, and expectantly. God has the power to turn a couple's "for worse" into "for better."

You might also want to exercise your wings of prayer for your loved ones, friends, and others you encounter who seem to need a renewal of physical, emotional, and spiritual strength. It can be one of the most exciting adventures of prayer you and your spouse have ever experienced.

Faith for Our Health

The prayer offered in faith will make the sick person well;
the Lord will raise him up.
JAMES 5:15

Lord God, thank You for creating our earthly bodies. We are grateful for our health and our sense of well-being. We pray that You would keep us strong and healthy so that we can better tend to our responsibilities and contribute to the work of the kingdom. We ask You to alert us when we are engaging in behaviors that hinder Your work in our bodies. Amen.

Health and Forgiveness

Confess your faults one to another,
and pray one for another,
that ye may be healed.
JAMES 5:16 KJV

Father God, we confess our faults to You and to each other. We let it all go, holding nothing back. We want to be clean and pure before You so that we might be healed and become worthy vessels of prayer for the healing of others. We honor Your will in all things. Amen.

Honoring God with Our Bodies

Don't you realize that your body is the temple of the Holy Spirit, who lives in you and was given to you by God? You do not belong to yourself, for God bought you with a high price. So you must honor God with your body.
1 CORINTHIANS 6:19–20 NLT

*L*ord, so often our health issues are the result of carelessness. Help us remember that our lifestyle choices affect our relationship with You. Our bodies are Yours. Help us make wise decisions and avoid harmful practices. Thank You, Lord, for offering us a fresh beginning every day. Amen.

Receiving God's Care for Our Bodies

The Lord cares about our bodies.
1 CORINTHIANS 6:13 NLT

*F*ather, it's good to know that You care about our bodies, and we understand that as a good father, You don't want Your children to be in pain or unable to exercise their gifts and callings. Thank You for creating us, and help us always turn to You when our bodies are not functioning as they should. Amen.

Healed and Forgiven

Praise the LORD, O my soul, and forget not all his benefits —
who forgives all your sins and heals all your diseases.
PSALM 103:2–3

*H*eavenly Father, thank You for forgiving our sins and helping us walk a path of new life. And thank You for hearing our prayers when we come to You for healing. We know Your purposes are known only to You, and sometimes You do not answer our prayers for healing in the way we expect. Help us to trust You and accept that You know more than we do. Amen.

The Great Physician

Jesus answered them, "It is not the healthy
people who need a doctor, but the sick."
LUKE 5:31 NCV

*D*ear Lord, You knew that we needed You long before we first realized it. You planned our rescue long before we knew we needed one. Thank You for looking down on us with compassion, for loving us even though we were marred by sin. We were in need of a physician, and You were there to heal us spiritually and restore us. Amen.

His Great Compassion

When Jesus landed and saw a large crowd,
he had compassion on them and healed their sick.
MATTHEW 14:14

*D*ear Jesus, when You walked here on earth, You touched so many and healed them of their brokenness, hopelessness, and disease. You touched the blind man and he was able to see. You touched the leper and he was instantly clean. You even raised Lazarus from the grave. Even though You no longer walk the earth, Your healing power remains. Heal us now, we pray. Amen.

His Name Is Healer

I am the Lord who heals you.
EXODUS 15:26 NRSV

*O*h Lord, Healer of Our Hearts, so often in our marriage we have a need for emotional healing. When two people live so close together, wounds are inevitable. Thank You for Your forgiveness when we fail each other. We are grateful for the healing that comes to our relationship when we submit ourselves to You. Amen.

Our Constant Provision

*Unto you that fear my name shall the Sun of righteousness
arise with healing in his wings. . .saith the Lord.*
MALACHI 4:2–3 KJV

Lord God, You are our constant healer, able to care for us in so
many ways. When our finances need healing, You are there to
give us the wisdom and self-control we need to get things back
in order. When our relationships need healing, You give us the
understanding and forgiveness necessary to put them back on
track. You are able to heal everything broken in our lives. Thank
You from the bottom of our hearts. Amen.

He Restores Us to Health

"I will restore health to you and heal you of your wounds," says the LORD.
JEREMIAH 30:17 NKJV

*L*ord God, living in this world is difficult. There is pain and sorrow, death and destruction all around us. Thank You for restoring us when we are hurt in battle and for showing us how to protect ourselves in the midst of the drama. You are a God who hears and responds to those who call on You. We are grateful to be Your children. Amen.

Life for the Body

A heart at peace gives life to the body.
PROVERBS 14:30

*L*ord, our hearts are often troubled in this wild and wooly world. So much is going on around us, but in the midst of it all, You offer us peace—the peace that comes from turning all our problems over to You. Thank You for keeping our blood pressure down and our heart rate regular as we trust in You. Amen.

Healed and Delivered

He sent His word and healed them,
and delivered them from their destructions.
PSALM 107:20 NKJV

*F*ather, so often we are hindered in our prayers for health and well-being because we have accepted negative thoughts and behaviors that crowd out the good. Deliver us from these destructive obstacles to Your healing touch. You are a kind and merciful God, and we trust You to help us turn our lives around. Amen.

Abundance of Peace and Truth

Behold, I will bring [my people] health and cure, and I will cure them, and
will reveal unto them the abundance of peace and truth [, saith the Lord].
JEREMIAH 33:6 KJV

*L*ord God, You are always looking out for us, always wanting to give us an abundance of Your peace. Help us trust that You will set us free from the ties that bind us to our old ways of thinking and doing. Cure us, Lord. Cure our hearts and heads as well as our bodies. Help us become well in every aspect of our being. Amen.

He Gives Us Full Life

*Worship the Lord your God, and his blessing will be on
your food and water. . . . I will give you a full life span.*
EXODUS 23:25–26

*F*ather, none of us knows how long we have to live on this earth.
One day, one of us will lose the other. When that happens, we
know You will be there to comfort the one left behind. But until
then, You have promised to give us full lives that can be used to
bless those around us. We know Your blessing is upon us as long
as we live. Amen.

Our Hope

The Power of Trusting God

May the God of hope fill you with all joy and peace as you trust in him,
so that you may overflow with hope by the power of the Holy Spirit.
ROMANS 15:13

*H*ope is that strong but gentle hand that keeps people moving forward when faced with uncertainty. The hope of recovery pushes patients to persevere through grueling physical therapy. The hope of freedom inspires refugees to continue journeying toward a distant shore. The hope of reconciliation provides couples with the resolve they need to call a marriage counselor when their cords of communication get tangled in a knot.

But it takes more than hope to yield results. A hope fulfilled is only as certain as what people are placing their hope in. People can hope to hit the jackpot, faithfully buying a lottery ticket every week, but their hope is placed on odds that don't support the chance that they will win.

The only hope that will always be fulfilled is hope in God and His promises. In the Old Testament, the people of Israel hoped that God would do the impossible—free them from slavery in Egypt, help them cross the Red Sea, and provide food and water in the desert for forty years. Joshua 21:45 testifies that "Not one of all the Lord's good promises to the house of Israel failed; every one was fulfilled."

Reading the Bible is a wonderful way to restore your hope when it seems all may be lost. Romans 15:4 says, "Everything that was written in the past was written to teach us, so that through endurance and the encouragement of the scriptures we might have hope." The Bible is not a textbook containing facts, figures, and rules that were recorded to be memorized. It's also not a storybook filled with myths meant to entertain or moralize. The Bible is unlike any other book ever written. Hebrews 4:12 says, "The word of God is living and active." God's Spirit gives the words of the Bible life, while prayer sets God's words free to be active in the world. These living and active words give those who read them the hope they need—a hope set firmly in the only One who can fulfill every promise He's ever made.

Achieving a successful marriage isn't all about simply finding the right person. What really matters is in whom you are placing your hope. Both you and your spouse are human. That means you'll make mistakes, disappoint each other from time to time, and probably break a few promises along the way—no matter how well-intentioned you are. But, if you place your hope in God and rely on His strong and gentle hand to guide you in learning how to love one another unconditionally, you'll find the courage and perseverance you need to forgive. Then you can continue moving forward, with the hope that your marriage will grow stronger as you continue to walk side by side.

Hope in God

Why are you cast down, O my soul, and why are you disquieted within me? Hope in God; for I shall again praise him, my help and my God.
PSALM 43:5 NRSV

Great God Our Helper, we place our hope in You—hope for a strong marriage, good lives, successful work, and an eternity in heaven. In fact, everything we are or ever will be is locked up in You. Without You, there is no future for us, but with You, we know our hope is well invested. We are so glad that You are our God. Amen.

Our Anchor

We have this hope as an anchor for the soul, firm and secure.
HEBREWS 6:19

Faithful Father, we thank You for being there for us through all the ups and downs of life. When times are bad, we can always look up to You for assurance of better days ahead. You kept us steady and strong in the valleys and on the mountaintops. Thank You for giving us hope. Amen.

Our Encouragement

*Everything that was written in the past was written to teach us,
so that through endurance and the encouragement of
the Scriptures we might have hope.*
ROMANS 15:4

*D*ear Lord, this life is pretty tough, but we can make it. We can be victors by trusting You. We have read in the Bible about people just like us who dared to trust You, and You never failed them. You even inspired many of them to write down their experiences, so we could be encouraged. Thank You for the hope that comes from the scriptures. Amen.

Our Savior

*We have put our hope in the living God, who is the Savior of all men,
and especially of those who believe.*
1 TIMOTHY 4:10

*F*ather in heaven, everywhere we look there is someone vying for our hope and trust—politicians, lawyers, doctors, and philosophers, just to name a few. Everyone says they have all the answers, but we know better. Instead we place our hope in You alone. You are the only one who has actually proven that You are worthy of our hope. Thank You. Amen.

Our Promise

*Put all your hope in how kind God will
be to you when Jesus Christ appears.*
1 PETER 1:13 CEV

*P*recious Father, we can barely wait for that day when the heavens open and You come for us. Right now it seems like a beautiful dream—the kind of dream we had as children when we imagined falling in love and getting married. We know that we are not dreaming in vain. We know that we can put our hope in that "one day" because You have never let us down. Amen.

Our Steadfast Love

Let your steadfast love, O Lord, be upon us, even as we hope in you.
PSALM 33:22 NRSV

*L*ord of heaven and earth, how is it that You love us? We can't understand and yet we cling to You, for Your words are backed up by Your actions. You have demonstrated Your awesome love by reaching down and saving us, redeeming us at an unspeakable cost. We receive Your love for us and give You back our own in exchange. Amen.

Our Unseen Reward

We hope for something we have not yet seen,
and we patiently wait for it.
ROMANS 8:25 CEV

Lord God, it seems like we are always waiting. We pray and expect to see an instant answer, but You are teaching us patience and endurance. You are teaching us that all good things will come at their appointed time. Sometimes we pray for each other and expect to see instant change. Help us to be gracious and caring as we wait for godliness to grow in each of us. Amen.

Our Heart's Keeper

He shall strengthen your heart,
all you who hope in the LORD.
PSALM 31:24 NKJV

Great God, You have come to dwell in our hearts, and now that You are there, we can't imagine our lives without You. How dark and dismal they would be. Thank You for choosing to live in us by Your Holy Spirit. His presence strengthens us. We are happy to place our hope in You. Amen.

Our Caregiver

Behold, the eye of the LORD is upon them that fear him,
upon them that hope in his mercy.
PSALM 33:18 KJV

Lord of heaven and earth, it's amazing to think that You dwell in us through Your Holy Spirit and also watch over us from heaven. You see and know our every need, our heart's every desire. You understand us from the inside out. Everything we will ever need is wrapped up in You. Thank You for loving us. Amen.

Our Portion

"The Lord is my portion," says my soul, "therefore I will hope in him."
LAMENTATIONS 3:24 NRSV

*F*ather, when we think of the word *portion*, it sounds like we are receiving an inheritance—a portion of Your vast kingdom. We are so happy to be Your children. You have given us so much. You have given us bright days ahead, fellowship with You, and the gift of each other. Thank You for everything. Amen.

Our Defender

No one whose hope is in you will ever be put to shame.
PSALM 25:3

*L*ord God, we have heard that it isn't wise to put all our eggs in one basket. At least that is what conventional wisdom says. But we have placed all our hopes, all our dreams, and all that we are in You. And we are not afraid. We know that You are completely faithful, and everything You touch is blessed. You will not let us down. Amen.

Our Compassionate God

This I call to mind and therefore I have hope:
Because of the Lord's great love we are not consumed,
for his compassions never fail.
LAMENTATIONS 3:21–22

*H*eavenly Father, we would be nowhere without Your love and mercy. If You had not treated us with compassion, where would we be? You looked on us, Your tainted creation, and You chose to fix us rather than throw us away. We are so grateful for Your compassion and understanding. Help us show compassion and understanding to each other. Amen.

Our Good God

The Lord is good to those who hope in him, to those who seek him.
LAMENTATIONS 3:25 NCV

*L*ord, we cannot imagine our lives without You. You are so good to us. Thank You for bringing us together and for putting love for each other in our hearts. Thank You for walking with us through the hard times and blowing on our flame of love when it was in danger of going out. Thank You for two lives becoming one and the blessing of Your hand as we work together through life. Amen.

Our Renewed Strength

Those who hope in the LORD will renew their strength.
They will soar on wings like eagles; they will run and not grow weary,
they will walk and not be faint.
ISAIAH 40:31

*H*eavenly Father, we have a great need for strength and endurance, love and patience, courage and fortitude, joy an fulfillment. The list is long. So many put their hope in the idols of money, success, and pleasure, even though these false gods offer nothing in return. We place our hope in You and receive abundance instead. We thank You. Amen.

Our Peace

The Power of an Unseen Kingdom

LORD, you establish peace for us;
all that we have accomplished you have done for us.
ISAIAH 26:12

A good marriage is a bit like ballroom dancing. To glide across the floor in a way that looks effortless to those around them, dance partners need to remain aware of their surroundings. They need to know where they are, remember where they've been, and know in what direction they want to move next. The dance of marriage requires the same kind of attentiveness. Being attentive in prayer can help couples become more aware of the big picture of their relationship: past, present, and future. Through prayer, God's Spirit reminds couples of what they've learned in the past and where they need to move forward and grow.

Right now, take a prayerful step back. Philippians 4:6 says, "Do not be anxious about anything, but in everything, by prayer and petition, with thanksgiving, present your requests to God." But there's more. This section of scripture holds both a call to prayer and a promise for those who pray. The verse that follows, Philippians 4:7, says that as a result of prayer, "The peace of God, which transcends all understanding, will guard your hearts and your minds in Christ Jesus."

God's peace differs from world peace or even from peace of mind. It is deeper and more enduring than an internal sense of calm and serenity. It can remain steadfast in the face of insurmountable difficulties. It is the calm in the eye of the storm.

When every anxious thought is bathed in prayer, the heart, the mind, and the life of the one who prays are transformed. Attitudes, perspectives, desires, hopes, fears, and relationships are all brought into the realm of Christ, where God's peace is paramount. When this happens, the one who prays is changed from the inside out, even if the outside circumstances remain the same. And as Philippians 4:7 makes clear, the miraculous power of this kind of peace is something that cannot be fully understood, either by those who see it from the outside or those who are experiencing its benefits firsthand.

Marriage takes more than two. It takes three: a husband, a wife, and an almighty God. God is the music you and your spouse are invited to dance to through life. Bound together in love and prayer, your relationship may look effortless to those around you, to those longing for a marriage where forgiveness flows, unconditional love grows, and a peace that transcends understanding prevails—a marriage that reflects the very heart of God. But you know the truth. It takes effort and attentiveness to stay in step with the peace of God through prayer. But like dancing, the more you and your spouse faithfully practice praying together, the more second nature it will become—and the more at peace you'll feel in every step you take.

Fixed on God

You will keep in perfect peace all who trust in you,
all whose thoughts are fixed on you!
ISAIAH 26:3 NLT

*L*ord in heaven, the world around us is swirling with words and images. Just flipping through the channels on television makes our heads swim. We need Your help to gain some peace in the midst of this bombardment. Even now, we focus our hearts and minds on You. We ask for Your peace and Your direction concerning what should be acted on and what should be left to Your care. Amen.

Knowing God

"Be still, and know that I am God; I will be exalted
among the nations, I will be exalted in the earth."
PSALM 46:10

*L*ord, we sense that before we can really receive peace and wellness from You, we must first get quiet and let You establish a place within us that's high above the thoughts of wars and disasters, rhetoric and propaganda, and the din of human existence. We ask You to bring a bit of heaven into our hearts—an oasis of peace in a troubled world. Amen.

The Reward of Righteousness

The fruit of righteousness will be peace;
the effect of righteousness will be quietness and confidence forever.
ISAIAH 32:17

*F*ather, we comprehend righteousness to mean "right living," and we believe that You command us to live in a way that will help us avoid painful circumstances that steal our peace and cause us pain and suffering. You are always looking out for us, working to make our lives better. We are so grateful. Amen.

Counsel Peace

Deceit is in the mind of those who plan evil,
but those who counsel peace have joy.
PROVERBS 12:20 NRSV

*P*recious Father, we are grateful for the peace You've brought to our lives. Show us how to spread that peace around in a world full of chaos and confusion. Bring across our paths those who are searching. Give us the words to tell them about You—the peace-giver—and what You can do in their lives. Amen.

Being Thankful

*Let the peace of Christ rule in your hearts, to which indeed
you were called in the one body. And be thankful.*
COLOSSIANS 3:15 NRSV

*H*eavenly Father, no organism can exist when it's fighting
against itself. We want to bring peace and harmony to Your
body of believers—those who have chosen to praise and worship
and obey You. Thank You for granting us peace in our hearts,
our marriage, and our fellowship with other believers. Amen.

Living in Peace

Aim for perfection, listen to my appeal, be of one mind, live in peace.
And the God of love and peace will be with you.
2 CORINTHIANS 13:11

God of peace, we are honored to be Your children, and we are grateful for the benefits that come with living our lives in obedience to Your commandments. We feel Your love and peace everywhere we turn—except when we turn away from the path You have prepared for us. Keep us on the road to peace. Amen.

He Is Our Peace

[Christ] himself is our peace, who has made the two one and has destroyed the barrier, the dividing wall of hostility.
EPHESIANS 2:14

Lord Jesus, we were once at odds with You, unfit for the kingdom, and unable to come into God's presence. But then You did something very awesome for us: You bought us peace. You paid the debt of consequences we had purchased with our poor choices and gave us access to God and His kingdom. "Thank You" is too little to say to someone who has given us so much. Please accept our humble praise. Amen.

Access to the Father

*[Christ] came and proclaimed peace to you who were far
off and peace to those who were near; for through him both
of us have access in one Spirit to the Father.*
EPHESIANS 2:17–18 NRSV

*F*ather, thank You for sending Your Son, Jesus, to do for us what
we could not do for ourselves. You sent Him to come and find
us and bring us back to You so we could know true peace and
true love. We do not take His sacrifice for granted. We thank You
with full hearts eager to please You in all things. Amen.

The Bond of Peace

*Make every effort to keep the unity of
the Spirit through the bond of peace.*
EPHESIANS 4:3

*S*weet Lord, so often we are the ones who disturb our own peace.
We let selfishness and willfulness break our unity and wreak
havoc on our lives together. We ask Your forgiveness for those
times when we have not protected what You have so graciously
given us. Create in us hearts that are prepared to hold on to Your
peace. Amen.

A Heart at Peace

A heart at peace gives life to the body.
PROVERBS 14:30

*H*eavenly Father, sometimes we feel stress wherever we turn—in our jobs, in our community, in our nation—even during our kids' sports events! We live in a competitive and fast-moving culture that is taking a toll on the health and well-being of our earthly bodies. Lord, teach us to cultivate peace in our home and carry it with us wherever we go. Amen.

Messengers of Peace

How beautiful upon the mountains are the feet of the messenger who announces peace, who brings good news, who announces salvation, who says to Zion, "Your God reigns."
ISAIAH 52:7 NRSV

*F*ather of Salvation, we can never repay You for all You've done, but we want to bless You by living our lives in a way that will testify to Your love and sacrifice. We want to take the message of Your Good News to everyone—the Good News that we are no longer at war with our Creator because we have been granted eternal peace through Jesus. Amen.

Going Home in Peace

You shall go out in joy, and be led back in peace;
the mountains and the hills before you shall burst into song,
and all the trees of the field shall clap their hands.
ISAIAH 55:12 NRSV

*L*ord God, we are excited about carrying Your message of salvation to others because we know that You will be by our sides, blessing and strengthening us as we go. It is a privilege and honor to tell others what You have done for us. Please accept our joyful praise. Amen.

The Prince of Peace

A child has been born for us, a son given to us; authority rests upon
his shoulders; and he is named Wonderful Counselor, Mighty God,
Everlasting Father, Prince of Peace.
ISAIAH 9:6 NRSV

*L*ord Jesus, there would be no peace on earth if You had been unwilling to leave heaven and become one of us. You lived a spotless life and then sacrificed it for our soiled and hopeless lives. We honor You this day as the Prince of Peace sent by the Father for the purpose of our restoration. May we always exalt You in our lives and in our marriage. Amen.

Even our Enemies

When the ways of people please the Lord,
he causes even their enemies to be at peace with them.
PROVERBS 16:7 NRSV

*L*ord God, we desire to be so close to You, so engulfed in Your presence, and so filled with Your peace that those around us feel the overflow. Friends and foes alike are disarmed by the spiritual atmosphere around us. That comes only by holy living. Give us hearts to seek Your commandments and live lives that are pleasing to You. Amen.

Our Future

The Power of Eternity

I know the plans I have for you, says the Lord, plans for your welfare and not for harm, to give you a future with hope.
JEREMIAH 29:11 NRSV

*T*he future of this world is constantly in question. There are wars, natural disasters, and financial upheavals—just a few of the dangers we can expect to see more of with each passing year. The wonderful news is that as believers in Jesus Christ, we have a far different future ahead of us. Will we suffer along with others through the hard times? Of course we will, but our God will sustain us. The difference is that our future extends far beyond the temporary trials we face here on earth. Our future lies with God. That means your future, both together and individually, will be bright, joy-filled, and eternal.

Though you may still wonder what the future holds, you will not be fearful. After all, you are not alone on this journey. You know who holds the future in His mighty hands. You know He cares for you and that He will never desert or abandon you. You know that His plans for your lives are sure and certain. And you know that death itself cannot keep you from receiving His promises and enjoying the wonders of eternal life with Him. Your faith will lighten the darkness ahead.

The two of you can go forward together through the years, always knowing that your future is bright. You need not fear anything because God is holding your hand and walking by your side. In exchange, He asks that you pray for those who do not yet know Him, those who are presently headed for destruction, and those who live in daily fear of what lies just beyond the horizon.

You have been learning to pray, and you can use the knowledge and experience you've been gaining to help others as well as yourselves. And in God's wonderful cycle of reciprocity, your prayers for others will return to bless you again and again. What an awesome privilege!

Open your hearts to pray for others. Ask God to send messengers across their paths that will speak to them about God's love. With God we have all things, but without Him, the future holds nothing of lasting value—only those things that can be lost.

Ask God to point out a married couple for whom you can diligently pray. Don't announce your intentions, but pray quietly and in the harmony of your own prayer chamber. Look for opportunities to speak words of truth and encouragement to them. Ask God to bless their future with the promise of eternity. Then thank Him for the promise of eternity in your own life.

A Prayer for Reverence

*There is surely a future hope for you,
and your hope will not be cut off.*
PROVERBS 23:18

*L*ord God, we praise, love, and honor You, and we look forward to the future You have put ahead of us. Through all our days and in all our ways, keep our hearts in humble awe, always ready to give You thanks for the blessings we receive and ever mindful of the reverence due to You, our God and Lord. Amen.

A Prayer for Righteous Living

*Consider the blameless, observe the upright;
there is a future for the man of peace.*
PSALM 37:37

*H*eavenly Father, thank You for the married couples we know whose faith in You and faithfulness to each other reflect Your will for husband and wife. Bless them, Father, and bless their years together. With these godly couples in mind, we come before You to ask for Your blessing on us, that we may exemplify righteous living and embrace our future in a spirit of peace and hope. Amen.

A Prayer for Revelation of God's Plan

As it is written: "No eye has seen, no ear has heard,
no mind has conceived what God has prepared for those who love him"—
but God has revealed it to us by his Spirit.
1 CORINTHIANS 2:9–10

All-knowing God, we often come before You to make requests concerning our future without even acknowledging Your special plans for us. We pray that the revelation of Your plans becomes our desire, and the truths of scripture become our hope and certainty. Replace our futile imaginings with the glorious reality of Your will for our lives together. Amen.

Our Confidence

You have been my hope, O Sovereign LORD,
my confidence since my youth.
PSALM 71:5

Heavenly Father, we have already come a long way in our marriage. You brought us together and have been teaching us how to trust You individually and as a couple. We are confident that You will continue Your good work in us. We will continue to hope in Your goodness and faithfulness. Amen.

A Prayer for Strength and Steadiness

My dear brothers and sisters, be strong and immovable.
Always work enthusiastically for the Lord for you know
that nothing you do for the Lord is ever useless.
1 CORINTHIANS 15:58 NLT

Lord Jesus, You have won the victory over sin and death, and our future life with You is assured. Now empower us with strength and endurance as we continue doing the work You have given us. We know there is nothing that can hinder or destroy Your eternal purpose, and we rejoice in our sure expectation of victory. Amen.

A Prayer for God's Will

Listen, you who say, "Today or tomorrow we will go to this or that city, spend a year there, carry on business and make money." Why, you do not even know what will happen tomorrow. . . . Instead, you ought to say, "If it is the Lord's will, we will live and do this or that."
JAMES 4:13–15

*D*ear Lord, the past, present, and future belong to You. Counsel us as we consider life's important decisions, and assist us as we share our dreams for the years ahead. No matter what, may Your will be done. Amen.

A Prayer for Vision

[Jesus said,] "I say to all of you: In the future you will see the Son of Man sitting at the right hand of the Mighty One and coming on the clouds of heaven."
MATTHEW 26:64

*A*lmighty God, through Your Word we have seen Your glory, and in Your promises we have placed our hope. Let the vision of Your mighty power strengthen us against the world's terrors. Help us comfort those overcome by anxiety, worry, and despair by proclaiming Your marvelous Word. Amen.

A Future without Worry

[Jesus said to his disciples,] "Seek first [God's] kingdom and his righteousness, and all these things will be given to you as well. Therefore do not worry about tomorrow, for tomorrow will worry about itself. Each day has enough trouble of its own."
MATTHEW 6:33–34

*D*ear Lord Jesus, You have told us not to worry and released us from our burden of anxiety. With the help of Your Holy Spirit, let us face the future with confidence in Your will and faithfulness. We live each day at ease in Your good providence. Amen.

A Future without Fear

[Jesus said,] "Give your entire attention to what God is doing right now, and don't get worked up about what may or may not happen tomorrow."
MATTHEW 6:34 MSG

*E*ternal God, we give thanks to You for delivering us safely to this hour. We are blessed to have each other and these moments to spend together praying and studying Your Word. Open our hearts to trust You with our future. We need not fear! You helped us yesterday, You are helping us today, and You will help us through each tomorrow. Amen.

Future Success

Good people can look forward to a bright future.
PROVERBS 13:9 NCV

*D*ear Lord, we know we reap what we sow, for that is the pattern You have set for the world. We ask You to send Your Holy Spirit into our hearts to sow Your wisdom and commandments. Let us look forward to a future of success, filled with the God-given fruits of honesty, integrity, faithfulness, family, friendship, productive work, and recreation. Amen.

Future Guidance

We plan the way we want to live,
but only GOD makes us able to live it.
PROVERBS 16:9 MSG

*G*od of all wisdom, we invite You to help as we make far-reaching plans and decisions concerning our home and family. Direct our thoughts, conversations, and analyses. Send us wise counselors and put before us the resources that we need to draw informed conclusions. Guide us, Lord, into our future days. Amen.

Thanks for What We Will Be

We are children of God, and what we will be has
not yet been made known. But we know that when he appears,
we shall be like him, for we shall see him as he is.
1 JOHN 3:2

*F*ather of all, we thank and praise You for calling us Your beloved children. As Your children, we put our reliance in Your Word and our trust in Your promises. As we rejoice in gratitude for all the blessings You have given us, we speak in heartfelt thanksgiving for all that is yet to come. Amen.

Thanks for God's Future Plan

The LORD's plans will stand forever;
his ideas will last from now on.
PSALM 33:11 NCV

*G*od of Our Days and Years, we come to Your throne with humble hearts to thank You for remembering us and blessing us with so many good things. We look forward to walking with You all our days, and we rejoice in knowing Your future plan for us is eternal life with Jesus Christ. Keep us, guide us, and protect us until that great day! Amen.

Thanks for Future Peace and Security

I am convinced that. . .neither the present nor the future, nor any powers,
neither height nor depth, nor anything else in all creation, will be able to
separate us from the love of God that is in Christ Jesus our Lord.
ROMANS 8:38–39

*U*nchanging God of the Universe, Your people have faced threatening circumstances and unsettling times. Yet they learned, as we are learning now, that You are still in control and still have compassion on us. With firm faith in Your protection, we give You thanks for our future of peace and security in You. Amen.

Our Joy

The Power of Rejoicing

The LORD your God will bless you. . .
in all the work of your hands, and your joy will be complete.
DEUTERONOMY 16:15

*C*omedians like to use the line, "I've been married for twenty years, happily married for five!" We all laugh and shake our heads because we know that marriage—like everything else in life—is a road with many twists and turns. Sometimes it's an amazing adventure, filled with exciting new things to see and explore. At other times, the road ahead seems boring and monotonous.

Marriage as God designed it, however, is intended to be consistently joyful. Rather than a source of stress, it is meant to be an oasis of peace in the midst of a tumultuous world. Rather than an emotional roller coaster, it is meant to be a sanctuary of serenity and reason during life's ups and downs. Rather than a temporary alliance, it is meant to be a permanent bridge over troubled waters. Your marriage is meant to be a refuge in hard times and a permanent joy.

Unfortunately, sin happened and set us all on a track of poor choices and selfish thought. These days, a wedded couple seems more like two camps living in close proximity to each other. They work together tentatively in between periods of outright hostility. Almost daily, one of the camps threatens to disassociate from the other in an effort to gain the upper hand.

Fortunately, we are not all doomed to living that way.

When God redeemed our sinful lives and gave us a second chance to be who He intended us to be, all His plans for us were reinstated—including His plan for marriage. Of course, God has not retracted our free will, so we will still be vulnerable to poor choices. But He has given us the Holy Spirit who lives in us and transforms us from the inside out. He has given us His written Word, too, where we can find courage and inspiration to live our lives for others rather than ourselves. And He has given us the power and privilege of prayer so that we can be participants in God's kingdom and His plans.

As you join hands and bow your heads in submission to your heavenly Father, you enter a new realm of surrender and unity. In that simple exercise, the two camps can come together and be governed by a new authority. Trusting each other transforms into trusting Him. Believing in each other turns into believing in Him.

Are you aware that when God redeemed you, He also redeemed your marriage? It's true! Your marriage won't be perfect, but you have some perfect tools to help you smooth out the road ahead and open your eyes to see the joy along the way.

A Prayer for Joy

To the one who pleases him God gives wisdom and knowledge and joy.
ECCLESIASTES 2:26 NRSV

*D*ear God, as we grow ever closer in our relationship with You through worship, Word, and prayer, we realize that You are the sole source of true pleasure in our marriage and in our lives. We commit ourselves to following You, for in Your way we find our path to lasting joy. Amen.

Doing Good

Serve wholeheartedly, as if you were serving the Lord, not men, because you know that the Lord will reward everyone for whatever good he does.
EPHESIANS 6:7–8

*L*ord God, thank You for the many opportunities we have to bring happiness to each other. Keep us committed to the daily kindnesses that make married life pleasant and joyful. Inspire us also to reach out to others with acts of caring, kindness, and consideration. Let us be there with friendly greetings, helpful hands, and understanding hearts. Amen.

A Prayer for a Joyful Soul

I will greatly rejoice in the LORD,
my soul shall be joyful in my God.
ISAIAH 61:10 NKJV

*L*ord God, we come before You in praise and worship—two souls rejoicing in the delight of knowing and loving each other and You. Keep us close to You, the wellspring of our joy, and let our souls find refreshment in the cool waters of Your love. Amen.

Agreeing with God

"Agree with God, and be at peace;
in this way good will come to you."
JOB 22:21 NRSV

*L*ord, all You've ever wanted is what's best for us, and yet, like spoiled children we still struggle against You at times. We think we know better where our happiness lies. But we are learning by hard experience that true joy comes from accepting Your will for our lives. Thank You for knowing us better than we know ourselves. Amen.

The Joy of Salvation

Yet I will rejoice in the LORD, I will be joyful in God my Savior.
HABAKKUK 3:18

*C*hrist Jesus, when life gets us down and circumstances bring us scant reason for happiness, remind us once again of the joy we possess in our salvation and in our relationship with You. Regardless of how the world changes, we stand on the firm foundation of Your unchanging love for us, and we are joyful. Amen.

Joy in Reconciliation

God was reconciling the world to himself in Christ,
not counting men's sins against them. And he has committed to us the
message of reconciliation. We are therefore Christ's ambassadors, as
though God were making his appeal through us.
2 CORINTHIANS 5:19–20

*H*eavenly Father, You sent Your Son, Jesus, to restore the relationship between Yourself and us. Help us respond in praise and thanksgiving as we become more and more like Him—willing to reconcile with each other, ready to work for peace in all our relationships, and eager to tell others about the light of Your love. Amen.

Already Winners

*In all these things we are more than
conquerors through him who loved us.*
ROMANS 8:37

*C*hrist Jesus, thank You for Your victory over sin and destruction. May Your life and resurrection be the joy that we cling to every day. Remind us that we are already winners through the life and work of our Savior, who continues to love and care for us. Amen.

Constant Rejoicing

*Rejoice in the Lord always.
I will say it again: Rejoice!*
PHILIPPIANS 4:4

*D*ear Lord, You invite us to come to You with our needs and desires, but You also urge us to simply rejoice in You. Help us turn to You daily for rest and refreshment. Give each of us a soul that delights in Your presence—a soul of constant rejoicing. Amen.

A Joyful Prayer of Thanksgiving

The Lord has done great things for us,
and we are filled with joy.
PSALM 126:3

*D*ear Father in heaven, when we begin to count all the blessings You have put into our lives so far—especially the gift of each other and our marriage—we cannot help but raise a joyful prayer of thanksgiving to You. Indeed, You have done great things for us, and may we never tire of sharing our blessings with others to the glory of Your name. Amen.

Joyful Restoration

"[A person] prays to God and finds favor with him, he sees
God's face and shouts for joy; he is restored by God to his righteous state.
Then he. . .says. . .'He redeemed my soul from going down to the pit,
and I will live to enjoy the light.' "
JOB 33:26–28

*S*avior God, what joy we find in Your message of forgiveness and restoration! As You have forgiven us and restored our relationship with You, so let us forgive one another and build back up our eroding relationship with others. With the power of Your Holy Spirit at work in our lives, let us never remain apart, but come together always in joyful restoration. Amen.

Joy in Our Wedding Vows

The third day there was a marriage in Cana of Galilee;
and the mother of Jesus was there: and both Jesus was called,
and his disciples, to the marriage.
JOHN 2:1–2 KJV

*L*ord Jesus, at the beginning of Your ministry among us, You blessed marriage with Your presence at the wedding feast in Cana. Be with us, too, as we celebrate the days and years of our marriage. Bless our holy union and our lives with the gift of Your love. With great joy in our hearts, we invite You to enter and live in our home. Amen.

Thanks for a New Marriage

With joy shall ye draw water out of the wells of salvation. . . .
Praise the LORD, call upon his name, declare his doings among the
people, make mention that his name is exalted. Sing unto the LORD;
for he hath done excellent things: this is known in all the earth.
ISAIAH 12:3–5 KJV

God of All Joy, You have given marriage as a gift of strength, comfort, help, and pleasure to men and women. Teach us, dear God, to live joyfully so our marriage will always be a blessing to us, our home, and our community. Amen.

Joy in Obedience

"Does the LORD delight in burnt offerings and sacrifices
as much as in obeying the voice of the LORD?"
1 SAMUEL 15:22

Almighty God, we pray for the wisdom to find genuine joy in obedience to Your Word. Let Your commandments guide our thoughts and actions, and let Your intention for marriage become the standard for our life together. Instill in us, dear God, a spirit of joyful obedience. Amen.

Joyful Trust in God

Let all those rejoice who put their trust in You;
let them ever shout for joy, because You defend them.
PSALM 5:11 NKJV

*L*ord God, protect us from relying on anything but You, for You graciously invite us to discover the joy of trusting You for all our needs and desires. You alone have the power to uphold us, and You alone know our truest needs. Together we commit ourselves to joyful trust in Your continuing love, protection, and care. Amen.

Conclusion

"Haven't you read," [Jesus] replied, "that at the beginning the Creator 'made them male and female,' and said, 'For this reason a man will leave his father and mother and be united to his wife, and the two will become one flesh'? So they are no longer two, but one. Therefore what God has joined together, let man not separate."
MATTHEW 19:4-6

God knows marriage is not easy. It is probably one of the greatest challenges of life, but He also knows that with His help the two of you can be more successful than you could ever have imagined. Together you will learn the joys of raising a family and making a purposeful life. You will learn to be kind and forgiving and put the needs of others before your own. You will learn to respect the truth and walk in it. You will learn to love and be loved with a tenacity that can only be called divine. You will see your weaknesses and learn how to match them to your spouse's strengths to form a strong and durable whole. Marriage will refine you and make you much better people in this life. And if that were not enough, it will also help you store up treasures in heaven.

Together you will find God's divine purpose and calling for your lives, becoming all He intended you to be, and then multiplying that exponentially. The words of Solomon in Ecclesiastes say: "Two are better than one, because they have a good return for their work." That is the promise of marriage, the heart of the principle of two becoming one.

As you become one, you will better understand how God

intended His people to become one with Him, individually and corporately. You will see with new eyes the depth of His love for you and the power of His personal sacrifice on your behalf.

And all the hope and promise that marriage brings comes together, expands, and explodes onto the scene through prayer. Yes, prayer is the key! Taking hands and speaking to God may seem like a simple, humble act—and it is. But it is an act with miraculous, amazing consequences far beyond your ability to even imagine! Open your hearts to each other, raise your eyes to God, and get ready to feel the earth move under your feet, for marriage is so much more than attraction and romance. When God joins two people together and they come before His throne in heartfelt prayer, they create a spiritual force powerful enough to move mountains. What a calling! What a privilege!